Cool
WORLD
COOKING

Fun and Tasty
RECIPES FOR KIDS!

Lisa Wagner

SCARLETTA JUNIOR READERS

MINNEAPOLIS, MINNESOTA

TO ADULT HELPERS

You're invited to assist up-and-coming chefs! As children learn to cook, they develop new skills, gain confidence, and make some delicious food. What's more, it's a lot of fun!

Efforts have been made to keep the recipes in this book authentic yet simple. You will notice that some of the recipes are more difficult than others. Be there to help children with these recipes, but encourage them to do as much as they can on their own. Also encourage them to try new foods and experiment with their own ideas. Building creativity into the cooking process encourages children to think like real chefs.

Before getting started, set some ground rules about using the kitchen, cooking tools, and ingredients. Most importantly, adult supervision is a must whenever a child uses the stove, oven, or sharp tools.

So, put on your aprons and stand by. Let your young chefs take the lead. Watch and learn. Taste their creations. Praise their efforts. Enjoy the culinary adventure!

The Lexile Framework for Reading® Lexile measure® 650L

Library of Congress Cataloging-in-Publication Data

Wagner, Lisa, 1958-
Cool world cooking : fun and tasty recipes for kids! / by Lisa Wagner.
     pages cm
Includes index.
ISBN-13: 978-1-938063-12-1 (pbk. : alk. paper)
ISBN-10: 1-938063-12-0 (pbk. : alk. paper)
ISBN-13: 978-1-938063-13-8 (electronic)
ISBN-10: 1-938063-13-9 (electronic)
1. International cooking--Juvenile literature. 2. Cookbooks. lcgft I. Title.
TX725.A1W24 2013
641.59--dc23

                    2012037042

Interior Design and Production: Colleen Dolphin, Mighty Media Inc., Minneapolis, MN
Cover Design: Anders Hanson, Mighty Media Inc., Minneapolis, MN
Editor: Liz Salzmann
Food Production: Frankie Tuminelly
Photo credits: Colleen Dolphin, iStockphoto (Steve Debenport, Rainbowphoto), Photodisc, Shutterstock

The following manufacturers/names appearing in this book are trademarks:
Argo®, Arm & Hammer®, Arrowhead Mills®, Betty Crocker®, Clear Value®, Crystal Farms®, Dei Fratelli®, Del Monte®, Fage®, Gold Medal®, Heinz®, House Foods®, Kame®, Kemps®, Kikkoman®, Krinos Foods, Inc.®, La Preferida®, Market Pantry®, Marukan®, McCormick®, Morton®, Oster®, Osterizer®, Old El Paso®, Old London®, Pyrex®, Roundy's®, Target®

Distributed by Publishers Group West

Printed and manufactured in the United States
North Mankato, Minnesota

 PRINTED ON RECYCLED PAPER

Table of Contents

Explore the Foods of the World!

Welcome to *Cool World Cooking!* This cookbook offers a great way to learn the basics of good cooking. Best of all, you will become a better cook every time you prepare a recipe.

I wrote this book because I wanted to share my love of food and cooking. I taught my own children about cooking before they could even talk! To keep my hands free for cooking, I put my first son in a backpack. He could watch over my shoulder and seemed very interested in what I was doing.

When I picked fresh herbs from my garden, I helped him learn each one. "Basil," I would say. "This is basil. We will use it in sauce for pasta. Smell it. Try a little taste. Now, we'll see if you can taste it in the sauce when it's done." He learned. He is an adult now, and he is an excellent cook!

So let's make it interesting and fun! When you use recipes from around the world, cooking can be an adventure, and making food from other cultures can teach you a lot.

You can learn about geography, climate, history, techniques, and traditions. Why does Mexican cooking use so many hot peppers? Peppers need a lot of heat to grow, so it must be hot there. Why do Italians use olive oil in everything? Olive oil is a heart-healthy source of fat, and Italy is filled with olive trees. Why do African recipes use peanuts? Peanuts are an excellent source of protein. Vegetable protein takes less water to grow than is needed to raise an animal. So, water must be scarce, and the weather must be hot. Why is there no pork in Middle Eastern cooking? The major religions of the region don't allow people to eat pork. See what I mean? You've already learned something about each of those places just by thinking about the ingredients!

In this book, you will find a lot of information to help you learn. The introduction for each region will give you background on the place, the people, and the culture. Pronunciation guides will have you saying the names of foods like a pro. You will also find pictures of foods and tools that might be new to you. For words you don't know, check the glossary. The index is helpful in many ways. If you want to find recipes that use rice, look up "rice" and you'll be all set. If you want to make Italian food, look up "Italy."

I hope that you will learn to love cooking as much as I do. Once you learn how to cook, you will always be able to make delicious food for yourself and others. So, let the adventure begin. Where will you travel first?

Lisa Wagner

The Basics

Get going in the right direction
with a few important basics!

ASK PERMISSION

Before you cook, get permission to use the kitchen, cooking tools, and ingredients. When you need help, ask. Always get help when you use the stove or oven.

GET ORGANIZED

- Being well organized is a chef's secret ingredient for success!

- Read through the entire recipe before you do anything else.

- Gather all your cooking tools and ingredients.

- Get the ingredients ready. The list of ingredients tells how to prepare each item.

- Put each prepared ingredient into a separate bowl.

- Read the recipe instructions carefully. Do the steps in the order they are listed.

GOOD COOKING TAKES PREP WORK

Many ingredients need preparation before they are used. Look at a recipe's ingredients list. Some ingredients will have words such as chopped, sliced, or grated next to them. These words tell you how to prepare the ingredients.

Give yourself plenty of time and be patient. Always wash fruits and vegetables. Rinse them well and pat them dry with a **towel**. Then they won't slip when you cut them. After you prepare each ingredient, put it in a separate prep bowl. Now you're ready!

BE SMART, BE SAFE

- If you use the stove or oven, you need an adult with you.

- Never use the stove or oven if you are home alone.

- Always get an adult to help with the hot jobs, such as frying with oil.

- Have an adult nearby when you are using sharp tools such as knives, peelers, graters, or food processors.

- Always turn pot handles to the back of the stove. This helps prevent accidents and spills.

- Work slowly and carefully. If you get hurt, let an adult know right away!

BE NEAT, BE CLEAN

- Start with clean hands, clean tools, and a clean work surface.

- Tie back long hair so it stays out of the way and out of the food.

- Roll up your sleeves.

- An apron will protect your clothes from spills and splashes.

- Chef hats are **optional**!

KEY SYMBOLS

In this book, you will see some symbols beside the recipes. Here is what they mean.

HOT STUFF!
The recipe requires the use of a stove or oven. You need adult assistance and supervision.

SUPER SHARP!
A sharp tool such as a peeler, knife, or grater is needed. Get an adult to stand by.

NUT ALERT!
Some people can get very sick if they eat nuts. If you are cooking with nuts, let people know!

EVEN COOLER!
This symbol means adventure! Give it a try! Get inspired and invent your own cool ideas.

No Germs Allowed!

Raw eggs and raw meat have bacteria in them. These bacteria are killed when food is cooked. But they can survive out in the open and make you sick! After you handle raw eggs or meat, wash your hands, tools, and work surfaces with soap and water. Keep everything clean!

Perfect Hardboiled Eggs!

Carefully set the eggs in a medium saucepan. Add cold water until it is one inch above the eggs. Bring the water to a boil, uncovered, over medium-high heat. Reduce the heat to medium and boil the eggs for 3 minutes.

Now cover the pan and turn off the heat. Let the eggs sit for 17 minutes. Then ask an adult to help you put the pan in the sink. Remove the cover. Run cold water over the eggs until they are cool.

Tap the large end of an egg on the counter to crack it. Remove the shell completely. Try holding the egg under running water while peeling it. This can make it easier!

Allergy Alert!

Some people have a reaction when they eat certain foods. If you have any allergies, you know what it's all about. An allergic reaction can require emergency **medical** help. Nut allergies can be especially **dangerous**. Before you serve anything made with nuts or peanut oil, ask if anyone has a nut allergy.

Salt and Pepper to Taste?

Some recipes say to add salt and pepper to taste. This means you should rely on your taste buds. Take a small spoonful of the food and taste it. If it isn't as salty as you like, add a little salt. If it needs more ground pepper, add some. Then mix and taste it again.

Herbs de Provence

Herbs de Provence is a special mixture of dried herbs. It includes thyme, savory, rosemary, marjoram, basil, oregano, and lavender. The mixture was invented in the Provence region of France. Herbs grow well in this sunny, southern region.

Now That's Hot!

Jalapeño peppers are very hot. Always wear rubber gloves when you chop jalapeño peppers. Then wash your hands, the cutting board, and the knife with soap and water right away. Be careful never to touch a cut pepper and then touch your eyes or nose. Ouch!

About Organic Foods

Organic foods are grown without synthetic fertilizers and pesticides. This is good for the earth. And recent studies show that organic foods may be more nutritious than conventionally grown foods. Organic foods used to be hard to find. But now you can find organic versions of most foods. Organic foods are more expensive than conventionally grown foods. Families must decide for themselves whether to spend extra for organic foods.

The Tool Box

A box on the bottom of the first page of each recipe lists the tools you need. When you come across a tool you don't know, turn back to these pages.

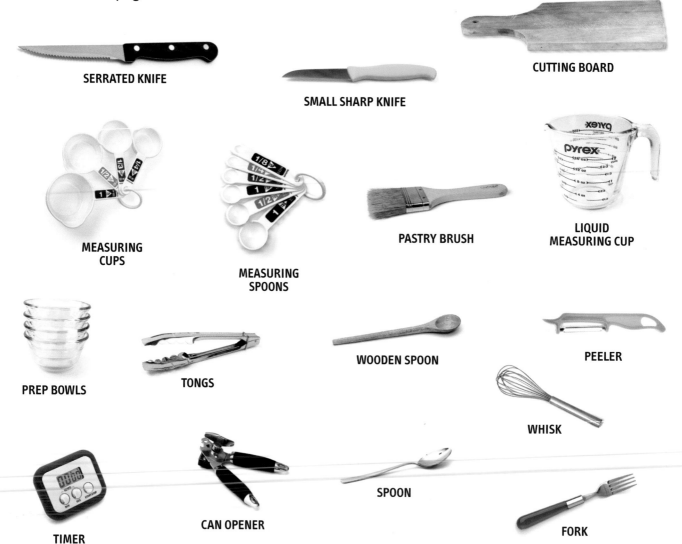

SERRATED KNIFE

SMALL SHARP KNIFE

CUTTING BOARD

MEASURING CUPS

MEASURING SPOONS

PASTRY BRUSH

LIQUID MEASURING CUP

PREP BOWLS

TONGS

WOODEN SPOON

PEELER

WHISK

TIMER

CAN OPENER

SPOON

FORK

JUICER

BAKING SHEET

DINNER PLATE/
SERVING PLATE

BLENDER

FRYING PAN

GRATER

SAUCEPAN

POT HOLDERS

SOUP POT

GLASS PIE DISH

SERVING BOWL

KITCHEN TOWELS

MIXING BOWLS

PAPER
TOWELS

9 × 9-INCH BAKING PAN

LARGE PLATTER

KITCHEN SCISSORS

STRAINER

SLOTTED SPOON

WOK

MEAT THERMOMETER

WIRE BAKING RACK

HAND MIXER

WOODEN SKEWERS

AIR TIGHT CONTAINER

RUBBER SPATULA

DESSERT BOWLS

14

SOUP BOWL

FRYING PAN WITH LID

ROLLING PIN

TABLE KNIFE

SALAD BOWL

PEPPER GRINDER

SMALL JAR WITH LID

KITCHEN STRING

SPATULA

PLASTIC WRAP

TOOTHPICKS

ALUMINUM FOIL

Cooking Terms

Here are some basic cooking terms and the actions that go with them. Whenever you need a reminder, just turn back to these pages.

FIRST THINGS FIRST

Always wash fruit and vegetables well. Rinse them under cold water. Pat them dry with a **towel**. Then they won't slip when you cut them.

CHOP

Chop means to cut things into small pieces with a knife.

GRATE

Grate means to shred something into small pieces using a grater.

JUICE

To *juice* a fruit means to remove the juice from its insides by squeezing it or using a juicer.

MIX

Mix means to stir ingredients together, usually with a large spoon.

MASH

Mash means to press down and smash food with a fork or potato masher.

SLICE

Slice means to cut food into pieces of the same thickness.

MINCE

Mince means to cut the food into the tiniest possible pieces. Garlic is often minced.

SAUTÉ

Sauté means to fry quickly in a pan using a small amount of oil or butter.

PEEL

Peel means to remove the skin, often with a peeler.

WHISK

Whisk means to beat quickly by hand with a whisk or fork.

MARINATE

Marinate means to soak food in a seasoned liquid.

SPREAD

Spread means to make a smooth layer with a spoon, knife, or spatula.

KNEAD

Knead means to fold, press, and turn dough to make it smooth.

CUBE OR DICE

Cube and *dice* mean to cut cube or dice shapes. Usually *dice* refers to smaller pieces and *cube* refers to larger pieces.

BLEND

Blend means to mix ingredients together with a blender.

GREASE

Grease means to coat a surface with oil or butter so food doesn't stick.

ARRANGE

Arrange means to place food in a certain order or pattern.

TOSS

Toss means to turn ingredients over to coat them with seasonings.

Explore the Foods of Mexico!

Are you ready to make some great Mexican food? Mexicans have been eating corn, beans, chiles, tomatoes, avocados, fruit, and fish for hundreds of years. Foods such as corn, chiles, and tomatoes grow well in Mexico. This is because of the long, hot growing season there. Avocados grow best on mountainsides. So if you think Mexico has mountains, you are correct!

When Spanish explorers came to Mexico in the 1500s, they brought new foods. These foods included rice, garlic, onion, spices, herbs, beef, **pork**, and **poultry**. The recipes in this book include some of these Spanish influences.

Spicy food is popular in hot climates because it makes people sweat. When a person sweats, he or she feels cooler. You will find chiles and chili powder used in this book. But don't worry! These recipes offer a little kick, not unpleasant hotness. Are you ready for a tasty Mexican adventure? Put on your aprons and off we go!

HOW DO YOU SAY THAT?

Enchilada (en-chee-LAH-duh)   Tomatillo (toh-ma-TEE-oh)

Guacamole (gwah-kuh-MOH-lay)   Tortilla (tor-TEE-yuh)

Taquito (tah-KEE-toh)   Tostada (toh-STAH-duh)

Ingredients

TOMATO

CELERY

ICEBERG LETTUCE

RADISHES

WHITE ONION

TOMATILLOS

BLACK BEANS

LIMES

AVOCADOS

CARROTS

GREEN BELL PEPPER

GROUND CUMIN

CHILI POWDER

GROUND CINNAMON

DRIED OREGANO

DRIED THYME

BAY LEAVES

JALAPEÑO PEPPERS

SALT

CILANTRO

GARLIC CLOVES

SCALLIONS

CHEDDAR CHEESE

MONTEREY JACK CHEESE

COLBY-JACK CHEESE

TOSTADA SHELLS

**VANILLA
ICE CREAM**

CHICKEN BROTH

DICED TOMATOES

**CANNED TOMATO
PURÉE**

DICED GREEN CHILES

CORN TORTILLAS

TORTILLA CHIPS

VEGETABLE OIL

OLIVE OIL

CANOLA OIL

SEMISWEET CHOCOLATE CHIPS

HEAVY CREAM

SALSA

GROUND BEEF

SOUR CREAM

CHICKEN BREASTS

Mexican Extras

Take your Mexican cooking to the next level! The ideas on these pages will show you how.

SUPER SHREDDED CHICKEN

Makes about 3 cups

INGREDIENTS

1 pound boneless, skinless chicken breasts
1 bay leaf
1 teaspoon dried oregano
½ teaspoon dried thyme
15-ounce can chicken broth

Tip: You can make more shredded chicken or ground beef than you need and freeze the leftovers! Remember too that beans are always a great meat substitute.

1 Put all the ingredients in a medium saucepan.

2 Bring to a boil over medium-high heat. Reduce the heat to medium and cook for 20 minutes.

3 Cover the saucepan. Turn off the heat and let the pan sit until cool.

4 Remove the chicken and rinse it with cold water.

5 Use a fork to shred the chicken.

GREAT GROUND BEEF

Makes about 2 cups

INGREDIENTS

1 pound ground beef
1 cup chopped white onion
1 clove garlic, minced
8-ounce can tomato purée
⅓ cup water
½ teaspoon salt
1 tablespoon chili powder
½ teaspoon dried oregano
½ teaspoon ground cumin

1 Put the meat, onion, and garlic in a frying pan. Cook over medium heat. As the meat browns, break it up with a wooden spoon. Cook until the meat is no longer pink.

2 Have an adult help you drain and **discard** the grease from the pan.

3 Stir in the tomato purée, water, salt, and spices. Cook over medium heat for 5 to 10 minutes, stirring occasionally.

GOT-TO-HAVE-IT GUACAMOLE

Makes about 2 cups

INGREDIENTS

2 very ripe medium avocados
1 small tomato, chopped
½ cup minced white onion
1 tablespoon fresh lime juice
¼ teaspoon salt

1 Cut the avocados in half and remove the pits.

2 Scoop the avocado from the skin and put it in a bowl.

3 Mash the avocado with a fork until it is mostly smooth.

4 Add the other ingredients and stir with the fork until blended.

MAJORLY DELICIOUS HOT FUDGE SAUCE

Makes about 1½ cups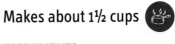

INGREDIENTS

½ cup heavy cream
⅓ cup water
12 ounces semisweet chocolate chips
1 teaspoon ground cinnamon
½ teaspoon vanilla extract
vanilla ice cream

1 Bring cream and water to a boil in a small saucepan over medium-high heat. Remove pan from heat.

2 Add chocolate and cinnamon. Stir until chocolate is melted and sauce is smooth.

3 Mix in vanilla extract until well blended.

4 Serve over vanilla ice cream.

Tasty Tostadas

Toasted tortillas topped with your favorite ingredients!

MAKES 12 TOSTADAS

INGREDIENTS

- ½ head iceberg lettuce, cut into ¼-inch strips
- 2 tomatoes, chopped
- 2 cups grated cheddar or colby-jack cheese
- 1 cup radishes, chopped
- 1 tablespoon olive oil
- 1 small white onion, minced
- 2 cups prepared shredded chicken or ground beef (page 26)
- 2 cloves garlic, minced
- ½ teaspoon dried oregano
- 2 tablespoons chili powder
- ½ teaspoon ground cumin
- ½ teaspoon salt
- ½ cup water
- 12 tostada shells

TOOLS:

small sharp knife	measuring spoons	wooden spoon	timer
serrated knife	measuring cups	baking sheet	serving plate
cutting board	grater	tongs	spoons and forks
prep bowls	frying pan	pot holders	

1 Preheat the oven to 350 degrees. Put the prepared lettuce, tomatoes, grated cheese, and radishes in small prep bowls. Set aside.

2 Heat the olive oil in a large frying pan. Add the onion and sauté over medium-high heat for 5 minutes.

3 Add the prepared chicken or beef and the garlic, oregano, chili powder, cumin, salt, and water. Cook over medium heat for 5 to 10 minutes, stirring occasionally.

4 Put the tostada shells on a baking sheet. Warm them in the oven for about 3 minutes. Remove from the oven and use tongs to gently put the tostadas on a serving plate.

5 Put 3 tablespoons of the chicken or beef on each tostada. Take the serving plate to the table. Set the prep bowls with the lettuce, tomatoes, grated cheese, and radishes on the table. Let everyone make their own tostadas just the way they like them!

Even Cooler!

You can add anything to your tostada! Try guacamole (page 27), sour cream, black beans, and rice!

Savory Mixed Salad

A simple dressing is this salad's best friend!

MAKES 6 SERVINGS

INGREDIENTS

- 1 head iceberg lettuce, washed and dried
- 1 green bell pepper, cut in thin strips
- 4 scallions, chopped
- 6 radishes, sliced
- 2 carrots, peeled and grated using largest holes on grater
- 1 avocado, chopped
- 1 tablespoon fresh lime juice
- 3 tablespoons olive oil
- ½ clove garlic, minced
- ¼ teaspoon salt
- ⅛ teaspoon chili powder
- 2 tomatoes, cut in wedges

TOOLS:
cutting board
small sharp knife
serrated knife

prep bowls
measuring spoons
juicer

peeler
grater
small mixing bowl

whisk
two forks
salad bowl

1. Put the lettuce in the salad bowl. Tear it into bite-size pieces.

2. Add the bell pepper, scallions, radishes, carrots, and avocado.

3. Put the lime juice, olive oil, garlic, salt, and chili powder in a small mixing bowl. Whisk until well blended. This is the dressing!

4. Pour the dressing over the vegetables and toss gently using two forks to mix.

5. Arrange the tomatoes over the top of the salad. Serve immediately.

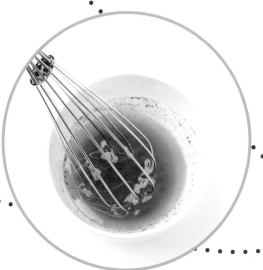

Amazing Mexican Rice

This rice makes a great side or main dish!

MAKES 8 SERVINGS

INGREDIENTS

1 cup long-grain white rice

2⅓ cups water

1 teaspoon salt

1 tablespoon olive oil

2 carrots, chopped

1 small white onion, minced

1 clove garlic, minced

1 stalk celery, chopped

14-ounce can diced tomatoes

1 teaspoon chili powder

TOOLS: medium saucepan with cover · cutting board · small sharp knife · prep bowls · measuring spoons · measuring cups · mixing bowl · kitchen towel · fork · wooden spoon · timer · can opener

1. Put the rice, 2 cups water, and the salt in a medium saucepan. Bring to a boil over medium-high heat. Stir.

2. Cover the saucepan and turn the heat to low.

3. Let the rice cook over low heat for 18 minutes. Do not remove the cover.

4. Turn off the heat and let the rice sit for 10 minutes. Then take the cover off the pan.

5. Use a fork to separate the grains of rice. Put the rice in a mixing bowl and cover it with a kitchen **towel**.

6. Wash and dry the saucepan.

7. Heat the olive oil in the saucepan. Add the carrots, onion, garlic, and celery. Cook over medium heat for 10 minutes, stirring occasionally.

8. Add the **diced** tomatoes, chili powder, and ⅓ cup water. Cook for 5 minutes, stirring occasionally.

9. Add the rice to the saucepan and stir to blend well. Cook over low heat 1 to 2 minutes, stirring constantly. Serve.

Tempting Taquitos

This amazing snack is too tasty to miss!

MAKES 9 SERVINGS

INGREDIENTS

2 cups prepared ground beef (page 26)

8 ounces Monterey Jack cheese, grated

18 corn tortillas

canola oil

salt

guacamole (page 27)

salsa

TOOLS: frying pan
tongs
paper towels

plate
medium mixing bowl
grater

measuring spoons
toothpicks
baking sheet

pastry brush
pot holders
timer

1 Preheat the oven to 450 degrees. Heat the frying pan over medium high heat. Lightly grease the frying pan. Just coat the surface with the oil so the tortilla won't stick.

2 Set a tortilla in the frying pan for 1 to 2 minutes, just until it is softened. Place it on a large plate and cover the plate with an upside-down mixing bowl. Repeat this step until all the tortillas are softened. Grease the frying pan from time to time as needed.

3 Take a tortilla and set it on your work surface. Put 2 tablespoons of ground beef and 1 tablespoon of cheese on the tortilla.

4 Roll the tortilla up and use a toothpick to hold it closed. Set it on a greased baking sheet. Repeat this step until all the tortillas are filled and rolled.

5 Brush each rolled tortilla (it is a taquito now) with canola oil and sprinkle with salt. Bake for 10 minutes. The outside should be **crispy** and the cheese should be melted.

6 Use tongs to set the hot taquitos on paper **towels** to drain any excess oil. Serve with guacamole and salsa for dipping. Taquitos are best eaten very warm right out of your hand.

Terrific Tortilla Soup

This zesty soup tastes great!

MAKES 6-8 SERVINGS

INGREDIENTS

2 limes, cut into wedges

1 cup sour cream

½ cup cilantro leaves

1 cup Monterey Jack cheese, grated

1 avocado, chopped

1 tablespoon olive oil

1 small white onion, chopped

3 cloves garlic, finely chopped

1 small can diced green chiles

4 cups chicken broth

28-ounce can diced tomatoes

½ teaspoon salt

½ teaspoon dried thyme

1 teaspoon dried oregano

1 teaspoon ground cumin

1 tablespoon chili powder

2 cups prepared shredded chicken (page 26)

1½ cups tortilla chips, broken into smaller pieces

TOOLS: cutting board · small sharp knife · prep bowls · measuring spoons · measuring cup · can opener · soup pot · wooden spoon · grater · timer

1 Put the prepared limes, sour cream, cilantro, grated cheese, and avocado in small prep bowls. Set aside.

2 Heat the oil in a soup pot or Dutch oven over medium-high heat. Add the onions and cook for 5 minutes, stirring occasionally.

3 Add the garlic and chiles and cook for 2 minutes.

4 Add the broth, tomatoes, salt, thyme, oregano, cumin, and chili powder. Bring to a boil. Then reduce heat to low and simmer for 15 minutes.

5 Add the chicken and simmer for 5 minutes.

6 To serve, put some broken tortilla chips in each bowl. Fill the bowls with soup.

7 Put the prepared ingredients from step 1 on the table. Let everyone **garnish** their own soup with the things they like best!

Tip

If you don't have time to make the shredded chicken, use roast chicken from a deli. Buy two ¾-inch slices. For this recipe, cut the slices into ¾-inch cubes.

Green Enchilada Casserole

INGREDIENTS

12 corn tortillas

vegetable oil for frying

12 tomatillos, papery husks removed

1 clove garlic, minced

½ teaspoon salt

6 stems of cilantro

3 cups shredded chicken (page 26)

2 cups grated Monterey Jack cheese

¾ cup sour cream

4 scallions, chopped

The first enchiladas were small fish wrapped in corn tortillas!

MAKES 8 SERVINGS

TOOLS: blender, saucepan, cutting board, small sharp knife, measuring spoons, measuring cups, grater, frying pan, plate, mixing bowls, wooden spoon, 9 x 9-inch baking pan, timer, pot holders

1 Preheat the oven to 350 degrees. Heat 1 teaspoon vegetable oil in a frying pan over medium high heat. Cook the tortillas one at a time for about 1 minute on each side. Add small amounts of oil as needed to keep the tortillas from sticking to the pan. Set the tortillas on a plate. Cover them with a medium mixing bowl to keep them warm.

2 To make the green sauce, put the tomatillos, garlic, salt, and cilantro in a blender. Blend until smooth. Put the mixture in a saucepan. Bring to a boil over medium-high heat. Reduce heat to low. Simmer for 10 minutes, stirring occasionally.

3 In a large bowl, mix the chicken, 1 cup of the Monterey Jack cheese, sour cream, and 1 cup of the green sauce.

4 Grease the baking pan.

5 Put ⅓ cup of the chicken mixture on a tortilla and roll it up. Place it in the pan seam side down. Repeat this step until all the tortillas are filled.

6 Pour the remaining 1½ cups of green sauce over the tortillas. Sprinkle the remaining 1 cup of cheese and the scallions over the sauce.

7 Bake uncovered for 40 minutes.

Even Cooler!

For a spicier sauce, chop up half of a jalapeño pepper. Add it to the green sauce. See note on page 11 about working with jalapeño peppers.

Explore the Foods of France!

French cooking is famous. Many of the world's greatest chefs trained in France. French cooking is an art and has been for centuries. Long ago, chefs who cooked for kings and queens wanted to be noticed. They worked hard to invent new dishes!

Today, the French are still serious about food. It can take hours to eat lunch! Most people shop for food every day in outdoor markets. Fresh food is one of the secrets to French cooking!

France has mountains, forests, valleys, and a coastline. These different areas offer a variety of **delicious** foods. Goats, cows, and sheep graze in the mountains. Mushrooms grow in the forest. Seafood and fish come from the coasts. Fruits, vegetables, olives, and herbs grow well in valleys too. Are you ready for a tasty French adventure? Put on your aprons and off we go!

HOW DO YOU SAY THAT?

Clafoutis (klah-foo-TEE)

Croque Monsieur (croak miss-YOOR)

Herbs de Provence (airb deh pro-VAHNCE)

Niçoise (nee-SWAZZ)

Pommes Anna (pawmz AHH-nuh)

Provence (pro-VAHNCE)

Quiche Lorraine (KEESH luh-RANE)

Ingredients

YELLOW POTATOES

RED POTATOES

WHITE ONION

SCALLIONS

PLUM TOMATOES

BLACKBERRIES

GARLIC

BLACK OLIVES

ROMAINE LETTUCE

GREEN BEANS

RASPBERRIES

FRESH PARSLEY

FRESH THYME

FRESH ROSEMARY

HERBS DE PROVENCE

FRESH DILL

FRESH OREGANO

GROUND PEPPER

KOSHER SALT

SALT

ALL-PURPOSE FLOUR

HALF & HALF

MILK

BEEF BROTH

EGG

SWISS CHEESE

GRUYÈRE CHEESE

FRENCH BAGUETTE

PREPARED PIE SHELL

BUTTER

BREAD

RED WINE VINEGAR

OLIVE OIL

VANILLA EXTRACT

CANNED TUNA

SUGAR

POWDERED SUGAR

DELI HAM

WHOLE CHICKEN

BACON

French Extras

Serve these with roast chicken or other main dishes!

GREAT GREEN BEANS FROM PROVENCE

Makes 6 servings

INGREDIENTS

2 tablespoons olive oil
1 small onion, finely chopped
2 cloves garlic, minced
1 teaspoon herbs de Provence (see page 11)
1 pound green beans, ends trimmed
2 plum tomatoes, chopped
salt
ground pepper

TOOLS

- prep bowls
- measuring spoons
- cutting board
- small sharp knife
- serrated knife
- frying pan
- wooden spoon
- pot holders
- timer

1 Heat the oil in a frying pan over medium heat.

2 Add the onions. Sauté for 5 minutes, mixing with a wooden spoon.

3 Add the garlic and herbs de Provence. Sauté for 1 minute.

4 Add the beans. Sauté for 8 minutes.

5 Add the tomatoes. Mix gently for 3 minutes.

6 Add salt and pepper to taste.

PERFECT POMMES ANNA

Makes 6 servings

INGREDIENTS

6 yellow potatoes, peeled and sliced
very thin
1 stick butter, melted
salt and ground pepper

TOOLS

- peeler
- cutting board
- small sharp knife
- small saucepan
- pastry brush
- 9 x 9-inch glass baking dish
- aluminum foil
- pot holders
- timer

1 Preheat the oven to 425 degrees.

2 Melt the butter in a small saucepan over very low heat. Remove from heat.

3 Brush a little butter on the bottom of the baking dish.

4 Put a layer of potatoes in the pan. Brush the tops evenly with melted butter. Sprinkle lightly with salt and pepper.

5 Continue to make layers of potatoes, butter, salt, and pepper.

6 Put butter on one side of the aluminum foil. Put the foil butter side down over the pan. Press it onto the potatoes.

7 Bake for 30 minutes.

8 Remove the foil. Bake for 30 more minutes or until potatoes are tender.

9 Remove from the oven. Run a knife around the edge of the pan.

Superb Salad Niçoise

This amazing salad is a meal in itself!

MAKES 4 LARGE SALADS

INGREDIENTS

- ½ pound fresh green beans, ends trimmed
- 4 small red potatoes
- 2 tablespoons red wine vinegar
- 5–6 tablespoons olive oil
- ¼ teaspoon salt
- ½ teaspoon ground pepper
- 2 tablespoons chopped fresh herbs (oregano, parsley, dill, thyme, or a combination)
- 1 head romaine lettuce, washed and dried
- 4 plum tomatoes, sliced
- 4 hard-boiled eggs, peeled and sliced (see page 10)
- 6-ounce can tuna, rinsed and drained in a strainer
- 20 black olives

TOOLS:
- saucepans with covers
- measuring cup
- measuring spoons
- small sharp knife
- serrated knife
- cutting board
- small jar with lid
- paper towels
- can opener
- strainer
- prep bowls
- timer
- 4 dinner plates

1. Boil the beans in 3 cups of water for five minutes. Drain them in a strainer and rinse with cold water. Refrigerate the beans until you are ready to use them.

2. Cover the potatoes with water in a medium saucepan. Bring to a boil, then reduce the heat to low. **Simmer** the potatoes for 15 minutes. Check the potatoes for doneness. A small sharp knife should go through the potato easily. If the potatoes are still too firm, continue simmering until the knife goes through easily.

3. Use a strainer to drain the potatoes. Rinse with cold water. Chill for at least 1 hour in the refrigerator. Then cut them into slices.

4. Put the vinegar, oil, salt, pepper, and herbs in a small jar with a tight-fitting lid. Shake until the ingredients are well blended. This is the dressing.

5. Divide the lettuce evenly between four dinner plates. Spread the lettuce leaves around each plate.

6. Arrange the potatoes, tomatoes, beans, eggs, tuna, and olives evenly over each plate of lettuce.

7. Pour some of the dressing on each **salad** and serve.

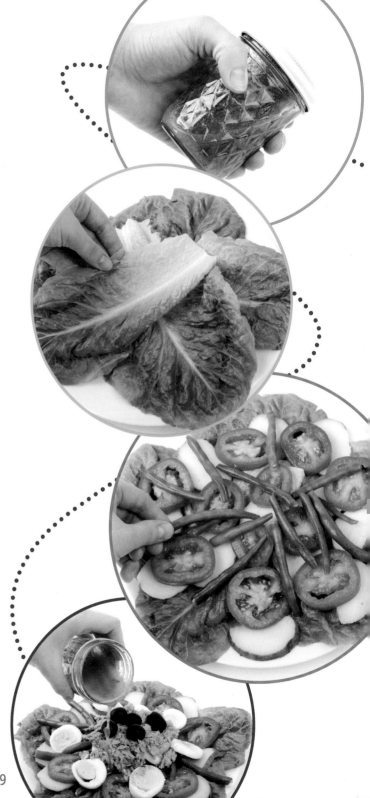

49

Fun French Onion Soup

Several great flavors all in one pot!

MAKES 4 BOWLS OF SOUP

INGREDIENTS

8 ¾-inch thick slices of French baguette

2 tablespoons olive oil

4 large onions, sliced into thin rings

4 cups beef broth

1 cup grated Swiss cheese

salt

ground pepper

TOOLS: prep bowls · cutting board · small sharp knife · grater · measuring spoons · measuring cups · baking sheet · timer · wooden spoon · soup pot · spatula · 4 soup bowls

1. Preheat the oven to 350 degrees.

2. Put the slices of baguette on a baking sheet. Bake for 5 minutes. Flip the slices over and bake for 5 more minutes. Remove from oven and let cool.

3. Heat the olive oil in a soup pot. Add the onions and cook over low heat for at least 30 minutes. Use a wooden spoon to mix the onions every few minutes. The onions are ready when they are deep golden brown.

4. Add the broth to the pot. Bring to a boil over high heat. Cover the pot and turn the heat low. **Simmer** for 20 minutes.

5. Divide the soup into four bowls. Put two slices of baked baguette in each bowl.

6. Sprinkle ¼-cup grated cheese over each bowl of soup. Serve with salt and pepper.

Even Cooler!

Add fresh herbs to this soup while it simmers. Use thyme, parsley, rosemary, or a combination of all three!

Classic Croque Monsieur

INGREDIENTS

4 slices of deli ham
½ cup grated Swiss cheese
4 slices bread
2 eggs
1 tablespoon half & half
2 tablespoons butter

A yummy French sandwich with a crunch!

MAKES 2 SANDWICHES

TOOLS: measuring cup   spoons   grater   whisk   spatula
measuring   prep bowls   mixing bowl   frying pan   pot holders

1. Put two slices of ham and half of the cheese between two slices of bread. Put the remaining ham and cheese between the other two slices of bread.

2. Whisk together the eggs and half & half in a mixing bowl.

3. Dip each side of the sandwiches in the egg mixture.

4. Melt the butter in a frying pan. Fry the sandwiches over low heat until they are golden brown on the bottom.

5. Use a spatula to flip the sandwiches over. Cook until the other side is golden brown and the cheese is melted.

Even Cooler!

Use herbed bread instead of plain white or wheat bread. Bread with rosemary or dill in it makes a **delicious** Croque Monsieur!

53

Lovely Quiche Lorraine

A perfect meal for breakfast, lunch, or dinner!

MAKES 4 SERVINGS

INGREDIENTS

- 1 unbaked, prepared pie shell
- 6 ounces sliced bacon
- 4 scallions, chopped
- 3 ounces Gruyére cheese (¾ cup grated)
- 4 eggs
- 1 cup half & half
- ¼ teaspoon ground pepper

TOOLS:

baking sheet	small sharp knife	pot holders	spatula
prep bowls	cutting board	timer	paper towels
measuring cups	fork	frying pan	mixing bowl
measuring spoons	grater	tongs	whisk

1 Preheat the oven. Follow the directions on the pie shell package.

2 Poke holes in the bottom of the pie shell with a fork. Put the shell on a baking sheet. Bake the shell for half the time recommended on the package. Take the shell out of the oven. Set the oven to 350 degrees.

3 Cook the bacon slices in a frying pan using medium heat. Use tongs to turn the bacon so it cooks evenly. When the bacon is lightly browned, remove it from the frying pan. Put it on paper **towels** to dry. Leave the bacon grease in the frying pan.

4 Cook the scallions in the bacon grease for 2 minutes. Remove the scallions from the frying pan. Cut the bacon into ½-inch pieces. Put the bacon, scallions, and cheese in the pie shell.

5 Whisk together the eggs, half & half, and pepper. Pour the egg mixture over the bacon and cheese. Bake for 30 to 35 minutes. Test for doneness by **inserting** a knife in the center. If the knife comes out clean the quiche is done. If there is batter sticking to the knife, bake for 5 more minutes. Let the quiche sit for 5 minutes. Cut into four pieces and serve.

Even Cooler!

- Add ⅛ teaspoon ground nutmeg for an **authentic** French taste!
- Use 1 cup of chopped cooked ham instead of the bacon.

Savory Roast Chicken

INGREDIENTS

1 whole chicken,
between 3 and 4 pounds

kosher salt

ground pepper

Simple to make and delicious to eat!

MAKES 4 TO 6 SERVINGS

TOOLS: baking sheet   kitchen string   meat thermometer
measuring spoons   pot holders   sharp knife
paper towels   timer   cutting board

1   Preheat the oven to 450 degrees.

2   Rinse the chicken inside and out and use paper **towels** to dry it. Sprinkle 1 teaspoon **kosher** salt and ¼ teaspoon pepper inside the chicken.

3   Cross the ends of the legs. Tie them together with a piece of kitchen string.

4   Put the chicken in the baking sheet with the breast side up. Sprinkle 1 tablespoon kosher salt over the chicken.

5   Put the chicken in the oven for 1 hour. Ask an adult to use a meat **thermometer** to see if the chicken is done. **Insert** it between the leg and thigh but not touching a bone. When the thermometer reads 165 degrees the chicken is done.

6   Take the chicken out of the oven and let it sit for 15 minutes. Ask an adult to cut the chicken into pieces.

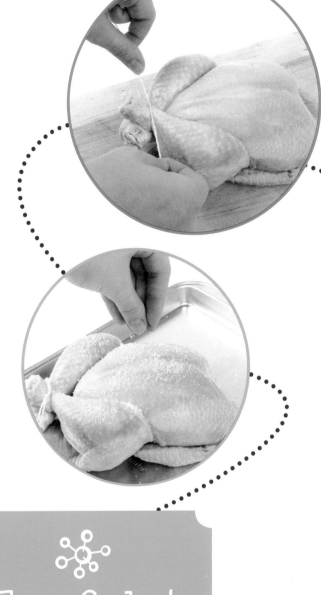

Even Cooler!

Make some amazing side dishes to serve with your chicken. Learn more on pages 46-47!

Very Berry Clafoutis

A sweet and creamy fresh fruit dessert!

MAKES 9 SERVINGS

INGREDIENTS

butter

3 cups fresh raspberries or blackberries

⅔ cup sugar

3 eggs

1/8 teaspoon salt

1 tablespoon vanilla extract

½ cup white flour

1 cup milk

½ cup powdered sugar

TOOLS: glass pie dish   measuring spoons   strainer   whisk   pot holders
paper towels   measuring cups   mixing bowl   table knife   timer

1 Preheat the oven to 350 degrees. Grease the bottom and sides of the pie dish with butter.

2 Wash the berries and set them on paper **towels**. Gently pat the berries dry. Arrange the berries evenly over the bottom of the buttered glass pie dish.

3 In a mixing bowl, whisk together the sugar and eggs for 1 minute. Keep whisking while you add the salt, vanilla, and flour.

4 Whisk in the milk. Pour the mixture evenly over the berries.

5 Bake for 50 to 55 minutes until the clafoutis is puffy and brown. Test for doneness by **inserting** a table knife in the center. When the knife comes out clean, the clafoutis is done. If there is a little batter sticking to the knife, bake for a few more minutes.

6 Remove the pan from the oven. Put the powdered sugar in a strainer. Gently wave the strainer back and forth over the clafoutis. Cut into nine pieces. Serve warm.

Even Cooler!

Use cherries instead of raspberries or blackberries. Wash the cherries and dry them gently with paper **towels**. Cut all the way around each cherry with a small sharp knife. Pry the halves apart and remove the pit.

Explore the Foods of Italy!

Do you like Italian food? Now you can learn to make it! Most people like spaghetti and meatballs. But they'll love the homemade **version** you can make from this book!

Food is very important in Italy. Dinners take hours to prepare and eat! The dinner table is the center of family life. Family meals often include grandparents, uncles, aunts, and **cousins**. "Put the love in the food" is a popular saying in Italy.

Many Italian cities and towns have outdoor markets that sell fresh foods. Northern Italy is known for its meats, cheeses, and grapes. Southern Italy is warmer. Vegetables, fruits, olives, and olive oil are produced there. Fish is harvested along the coasts of the Mediterranean.

HOW DO YOU SAY THAT?

Insalata Mista
(EEN-sah-LAH-tah MEE-stah)

Granita (grah-NEE-tah)

Parmigiana (pahr-muh-ZHAH-nuh)

Lasagna (luh-ZAHN-yuh)

Napoli (NAH-poh-lee)

Ingredients

TOMATO

CELERY

WHITE ONION

SCALLIONS

GREEN BEANS

LEMONS

FIELD GREENS

RED BELL PEPPER

CARROTS

SHALLOTS

FRESH ITALIAN PARSLEY

BIBB LETTUCE

GARLIC

FENNEL SEED

DRIED OREGANO

DRIED BASIL

BROWN SUGAR

SPAGHETTI NOODLES

NUTMEG

FETTUCCINE NOODLES

NO-BOIL LASAGNA NOODLES

ITALIAN BREAD

ITALIAN SAUSAGE

CRUSHED TOMATOES

HEAVY WHIPPING CREAM

EGG

GROUND BEEF

PARMESAN CHEESE

MOZZARELLA CHEESE

RICOTTA CHEESE

GROUND PEPPER

OLIVE OIL

**RED WINE
VINEGAR**

BREAD CRUMBS

SUGAR

SALT

BUTTER

Italian Extras

Take your Italian cooking to the next level! The ideas on these pages will show you how.

PERFECT PASTA EVERY TIME!

Different kinds of pasta have different cook times. The suggested cooking time is always on the package.

1 Put 4 quarts of water in a heavy-bottomed saucepan. Add 1 tablespoon of salt and stir until it is **dissolved**.

2 Bring the water to a boil over high heat. The entire surface of the water should be bubbling. Add the pasta and stir gently.

3 Wait for the water to begin boiling again. Then set the timer for the time shown on the package. Boil the pasta uncovered and stir it every few minutes. Make sure the pasta doesn't stick to the bottom of the pan.

4 Set a colander in the sink. Pour the pasta into the colander to drain. Serve immediately with sauce.

GORGEOUS GARLIC BREAD

Makes 8 to 12 servings

INGREDIENTS

18-inch loaf soft Italian bread
12 tablespoons softened butter
5 cloves garlic, minced
1 cup Parmesan cheese, grated

1 Preheat the oven to 350 degrees. Slice the bread lengthwise. Don't cut through all the way.

2 Mix the butter, garlic, and Parmesan cheese in a bowl. Spread the mixture evenly on both sides of the bread.

3 Close the loaf. Slice it into 1-inch pieces. Don't cut all the way through. Wrap the loaf in aluminum foil. Set it on a baking sheet. Bake for 15 minutes.

4 Carefully unwrap the bread and finish slicing though each cut to separate the pieces.

REMARKABLE RED SAUCE

Makes about 3 quarts

INGREDIENTS

2 tablespoons olive oil
1 pound bulk Italian sausage
1 large onion, chopped
3 cloves garlic, minced
3 28-ounce cans crushed tomatoes
¾ cup water
1 teaspoon fennel seed
1 teaspoon dried basil
1 teaspoon dried oregano
1 teaspoon salt
¼ teaspoon ground pepper
1 tablespoon brown sugar

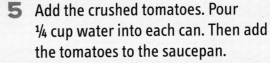

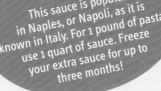

Tip:
This sauce is popular in Naples, or Napoli, as it is known in Italy. For 1 pound of pasta, use 1 quart of sauce. Freeze your extra sauce for up to three months!

1 Heat the olive oil in a large saucepan over medium heat. Add the sausage and break it up using a wooden spoon. Cook it until all the pink is gone.

2 Move the sausage to a bowl using a slotted spoon. Set it aside.

3 Add the onion and garlic to the saucepan and sauté for 5 minutes, stirring constantly.

4 Add the sausage to the onion and garlic.

5 Add the crushed tomatoes. Pour ¼ cup water into each can. Then add the tomatoes to the saucepan.

6 Add the herbs, salt, and pepper. Stir to blend.

7 Bring the sauce to a boil over medium-high heat, stirring often.

8 Reduce the heat and let the sauce cook over low heat for 1 hour, stirring often.

9 Stir in the brown sugar.

10 Serve this sauce over any cooked pasta.

Fantastic Fettuccine Alfredo

Fettuccine means "little ribbons" in Italian!

MAKES 4 SERVINGS

INGREDIENTS

- salt
- 2 tablespoons butter
- 1 large shallot, minced
- 2 cups heavy whipping cream
- ½ cup grated Parmesan cheese
- ¼ teaspoon ground pepper
- 1/8 teaspoon nutmeg
- 8 ounces fettuccine noodles
- ¼ cup chopped Italian parsley

TOOLS: prep bowls, grater, cutting board, small sharp knife, heavy-bottomed saucepan, measuring spoons, measuring cups, medium saucepan, wooden spoon, timer, pot holders, strainer, serving bowl

1. Put 4 quarts of water in a large heavy-bottomed saucepan. Add 1 tablespoon of salt. Stir to **dissolve** the salt. Cover the pot and bring the water to a boil.

2. Meanwhile, heat the butter in a medium saucepan over medium-high heat.

3. When the butter is melted, add the shallot. Sauté over medium heat for 3 minutes, stirring with a wooden spoon.

4. Turn down the heat. Stir in the cream, Parmesan cheese, ¼ teaspoon salt, pepper, and nutmeg. Cook over low heat for 5 minutes, stirring often.

5. Add the fettuccine noodles to the boiling water. The package will tell you how long to boil the noodles. See page 66 for more information about cooking pasta.

6. While the fettuccine cooks, continue cooking the sauce over low heat, stirring often.

7. Drain the fettuccine in a strainer. Then put it in a large serving bowl. Pour the sauce over the fettuccine. Stir to coat the pasta with the sauce. Let stand for 5 minutes.

8. Sprinkle with parsley and serve.

Green Beans Parmigiana

Anything with Parmesan cheese
can be called Parmigiana!

MAKES 6 SERVINGS

INGREDIENTS

- salt
- 1 pound green beans, ends trimmed off
- 2 tablespoons butter
- 2 tablespoons olive oil
- ½ cup Parmesan cheese, grated
- ground pepper

TOOLS:

prep bowls	grater	large saucepan	wooden spoon
cutting board	measuring spoons	strainer	serving bowl
small sharp knife	measuring cups	large frying pan	

1 Fill a large saucepan halfway with water. Add 1 tablespoon of salt and stir to **dissolve**.

2 Bring the water to a boil and add the green beans.

3 Boil the beans uncovered for 4 to 5 minutes. The beans should be crisp yet tender and bright green.

4 Drain the beans using a strainer. Run cold water over them to stop the cooking process.

5 Put the olive oil and butter in a large frying pan. Heat over medium-high heat until the butter is melted.

6 Add the beans and sauté for 3 minutes, stirring constantly.

7 Put the beans in a serving bowl. Add salt and pepper to taste. Sprinkle with Parmesan cheese and serve.

Legendary Lasagna

Lasagna means "cooking pot" in Latin. So this dish is named after a dish!

MAKES ABOUT 8 SERVINGS

INGREDIENTS

- 4 cups prepared Remarkable Red Sauce (see page 67)
- 3 cups ricotta cheese
- 2 eggs
- 1 cup Parmesan cheese, grated
- ¼ cup Italian parsley, chopped
- 9-ounce package no-boil lasagna noodles
- 8 ounces mozzarella cheese, grated
- olive oil

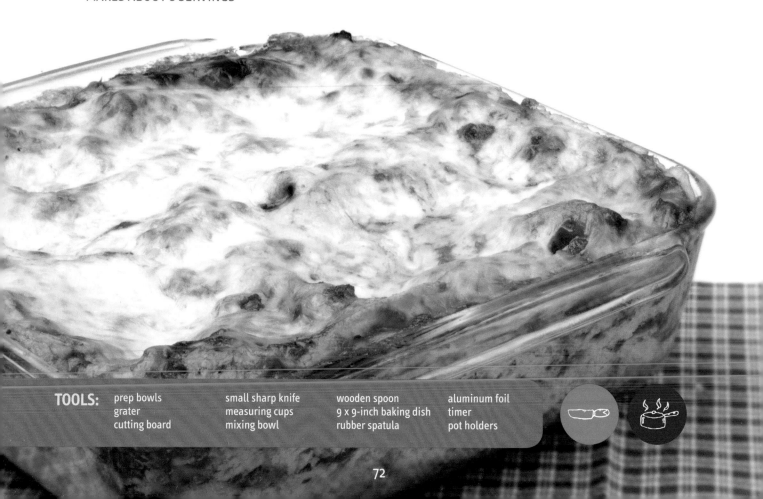

TOOLS: prep bowls, grater, cutting board, small sharp knife, measuring cups, mixing bowl, wooden spoon, 9 x 9-inch baking dish, rubber spatula, aluminum foil, timer, pot holders

1 Follow the steps on page 67 to prepare the red sauce. Don't add the sausage. Preheat the oven to 400 degrees.

2 Put all the remaining ingredients except the noodles in a large mixing bowl. Using your hands, blend all the ingredients together. Wash your hands first!

3 Get your hands wet. Roll some of the mixture between your hands to make a meatball. It should be about 1½ inches across.

4 Put the meatball on a baking sheet. Make more meatballs until you have used all of the mixture. Bake the meatballs for 25 minutes.

5 Check the meatballs for doneness. Cut one in half. Make sure it is not still pink inside. If the meatballs are not done, bake for 5 more minutes.

6 Combine the meatballs and the red sauce in a large saucepan. Cook over medium heat for 30 minutes.

7 Meanwhile, prepare the spaghetti noodles. Follow the steps on page 66.

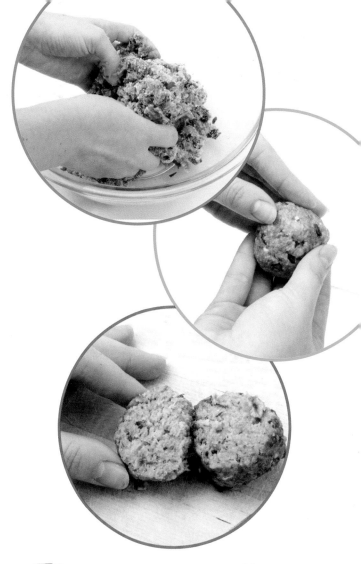

Tip

You can make the meatballs ahead of time! Then store them in the refrigerator in a zip top bag. You need to use them within a day or two. Or you can freeze the meatballs for up to three months. Wrap the zip top bag in two layers of aluminum foil. When you are ready to use the meatballs, let them thaw in the refrigerator for 24 hours. Then follow step 6 to reheat them in the sauce.

Impressive Insalata Mista

Italy's version of a mixed salad!

MAKES 6-8 SERVINGS

INGREDIENTS

- 1 garlic clove, cut in half
- 1 head Bibb lettuce, washed and dried
- 1 red bell pepper, cut into thin strips
- 4 scallions, chopped
- 6 ounces field greens
- 1 stalk celery, cut into thin slices
- 2 carrots, peeled and grated using largest holes on grater
- 1 tablespoon fresh lemon juice
- 3 tablespoons olive oil
- 2 tomatoes, cut into wedges
- 2 teaspoons red wine vinegar
- salt
- ground pepper

TOOLS: cutting board, small sharp knife, serrated knife, prep bowls, measuring spoons, juicer, peeler, grater, two forks, salad bowl

1. Rub a large salad bowl with the garlic. Leave the garlic in the bowl.

2. Put the lettuce in the bowl. Tear it into bite-size pieces. Add the bell pepper, scallions, field greens, celery, and carrots.

3. Sprinkle the lemon juice over the salad and toss gently to mix. Sprinkle the olive oil over the salad and toss again.

4. Add the tomatoes. Sprinkle red wine vinegar over the salad. Toss gently with two forks to mix.

5. Remove the garlic. Add salt and pepper to taste. Serve immediately.

Even Cooler!

Try using other types of lettuce such as butter lettuce, Romaine lettuce, or leaf lettuce. You could also use cherry tomatoes instead of whole tomatoes. Or add sliced radishes, green bell pepper, or mushrooms.

Tangy Lemon Granita

INGREDIENTS

3 cups water
1¼ cups sugar
1 cup fresh lemon juice

*It takes six hours,
but every bite is worth it!*

MAKES 6 SERVINGS

TOOLS: prep bowl   small saucepan   pot holders   fork
juicer   wooden spoon   round glass baking   dessert bowls
measuring cups   timer   dish

1. Start making the granita at least six hours before serving. Put the water and sugar in a small saucepan over high heat. Use a wooden spoon to stir until the sugar is **dissolved**.

2. Bring the mixture to a boil and cook for 5 minutes. Remove the pan from the heat. Let the mixture stand for 5 minutes.

3. Add the lemon juice and stir to mix. Let the mixture cool for 20 minutes.

4. Pour the mixture into the baking dish. Put the dish in the freezer.

5. Remove the dish from the freezer after 2 hours. The mixture will be slushy. Use a fork to mash it and mix the frozen and unfrozen parts. Put the dish back in the freezer.

6. Repeat the mashing and mixing every hour for the next 4 hours. Put it in dessert bowls to serve.

Tip

You can make the granita ahead of time. After Step 6, leave the granita in the baking dish. Cover the dish with plastic wrap. Put it back in the freezer. Take it out 15 minutes before you want to serve the granita. Use a fork to mash and mix one more time. Then put it in the dessert bowls.

Even Cooler!

Try making granita with juice from oranges or pink grapefruit. You can also make granita from bottled juice. If the juice is already sweetened, pour it into the baking dish. Begin at step 4.

Explore the Foods of Africa!

Africa is the second-largest continent. It has more than 50 countries. The people speak more than 1,000 different languages! There are also magnificent mountains, jungles, deserts, tropical rainforests, and miles of coastline.

Most Africans eat more fruits and vegetables than meat. Fish is **available** along the coasts. A lot of different fruits are grown in the tropical areas. Yams, rice, corn, onions, tomatoes, and chili peppers are common in hot, dry areas.

African cooking varies by region. In this book, we will explore recipes from Algeria and Morocco in the north, Ethiopia and Kenya in the east, and Ivory Coast and Liberia in the west.

Substitutions are common in African cooking. People cook with what is **available**! A creative cook can make a **delicious** stew with a few vegetables, a little water, and some spices! It's called **improvising**! Are you ready for a tasty African adventure? Put on your apron and off we go!

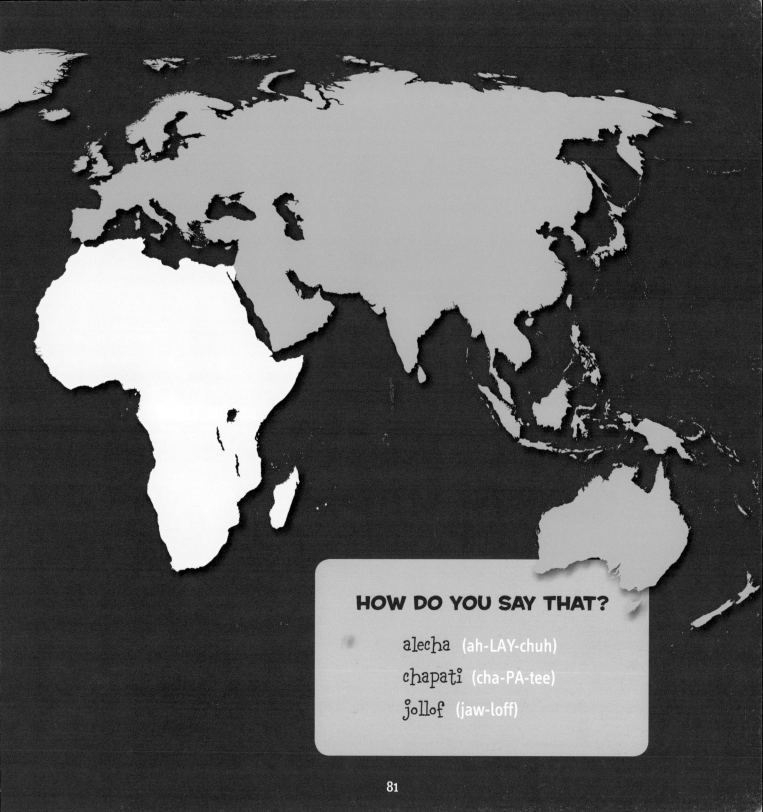

HOW DO YOU SAY THAT?

alecha (ah-LAY-chuh)

chapati (cha-PA-tee)

jollof (jaw-loff)

Ingredients

GREEN BEANS

WHITE ONION

POTATOES

SWEET POTATO

CARROTS

GINGER ROOT

ZUCCHINI

CABBAGE

GREEN BELL PEPPER

RED BELL PEPPER

SCALLIONS

OKRA

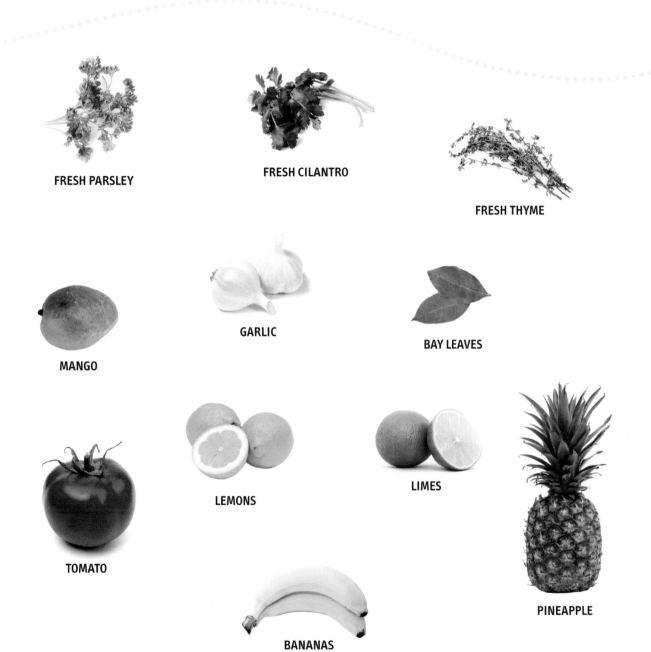

FRESH PARSLEY

FRESH CILANTRO

FRESH THYME

MANGO

GARLIC

BAY LEAVES

TOMATO

LEMONS

LIMES

PINEAPPLE

BANANAS

CAYENNE PEPPER

GROUND PEPPER

GROUND CUMIN

LONG-GRAIN RICE

PAPRIKA

TOMATO SAUCE

CANNED WHOLE TOMATOES

CANNED MIXED TROPICAL FRUIT

CHICKEN BROTH

CHICKPEAS

**RED WINE
VINEGAR**

OLIVE OIL

ALL-PURPOSE FLOUR

CANOLA OIL

PEANUT BUTTER

SALT

CHICKEN BREASTS

SHREDDED COCONUT

African Extras

Take your African cooking to the next level! The ideas on these pages will show you how.

CRUNCHY CABBAGE SALAD

Makes 8 servings

INGREDIENTS
½ cabbage, sliced very thin
3 carrots, peeled and grated
15-ounce can mixed tropical fruit, drained
juice from 1 lime
¼ teaspoon salt
3 tablespoons canola oil

1   Put the cabbage, carrots, and tropical fruit in a salad bowl. Mix well.

2   In mixing bowl, whisk the lime juice, salt, and oil together. Pour the mixture over the salad and mix well. Cover and refrigerate for an hour before serving.

PERFECTLY COOKED RICE

Makes 4 to 6 servings

INGREDIENTS
3 cups water
1½ cups long-grain rice
1 teaspoon salt

1   Combine water, rice, and salt in a saucepan. Bring to a boil.

2   Cover the pan when little holes appear between the grains of rice. This should take about 8 minutes. The surface of the rice will also look a little dry.

3   Turn the heat down to very low. Cook the rice for 15 more minutes.

4   Remove the pan from the heat. Let the rice stand, covered, for 5 minutes.

5   Fluff the rice with a fork before serving.

FANTASTIC CHAPATI FLATBREAD

Makes 4 chapati

INGREDIENTS

2 cups all-purpose flour
1 teaspoon salt
2/3 cup warm water
2 teaspoons canola oil

1 Put the flour and salt in a mixing bowl. Mix them with a fork.

2 Slowly add the warm water. Mix with your hands. Make sure you wash them first! As you mix, it will start to turn into dough. If the mixture doesn't become a thick dough, add 1 teaspoon of warm water. Then mix it some more. Keep adding warm water 1 tablespoon at a time. Mix well after each time. Stop when the dough is thick.

3 Mix in the canola oil.

4 Sprinkle some flour on a cutting board. Use only enough flour to keep the dough from sticking. Knead the dough until is a smooth ball. Put it in a bowl.

5 Cover the bowl with a clean kitchen **towel**. Let the dough rest for 30 minutes.

6 Divide the dough into four equal pieces. Shape each piece into a ball.

7 Sprinkle more flour on the cutting board as needed. Use a rolling pin to flatten each ball of dough. They should each be about 6 to 7 inches across. You can also flatten the dough by hand.

8 Put 1 teaspoon of oil in a frying pan. Heat over medium-high heat until the oil is hot.

9 Put one piece of dough in the pan. Fry it for 3 minutes on one side. Then flip the chapati with a spatula. Fry it for 3 minutes on the second side. Each side of the chapati should have golden brown marks on it. If the dough gets burned spots, turn down the heat.

10 Remove the chapati and put it on a plate. Cover it with a clean kitchen towel while you fry the next one.

11 Repeat Steps 8 through 10 until all the dough is fried.

Seasoned Chickpea Salad

A healthy and tasty Algerian dish chock full of flavor!

MAKES 6 TO 8 SERVINGS

INGREDIENTS

- 4 tablespoons olive oil
- 1 tablespoon red wine vinegar
- 1 tablespoon lemon juice
- ¾ cup finely chopped parsley
- ½ teaspoon salt
- ¼ teaspoon ground pepper
- 2 15-ounce cans chickpeas, rinsed and drained
- 1 white onion (about 3 inches across), minced
- 4 scallions, chopped

TOOLS: juicer | measuring cups | can opener | whisk
prep bowls | cutting board | strainer | wooden spoon
measuring spoons | small sharp knife | large mixing bowl

1 Put the olive oil, vinegar, and lemon juice in a large mixing bowl. Whisk them together. Add the parsley, salt, and pepper. Whisk to blend.

2 Add the chickpeas, onion, and scallions. Mix well with a wooden spoon.

3 Chill for at least 1 hour before serving.

Even Cooler!

Use ½ cup finely chopped cilantro instead of the parsley. Also add 1 teaspoon ground cumin.

Sizzling Groundnut Stew

A wonderful West African specialty for lunch or dinner!

MAKES 4 TO 6 SERVINGS

TOOLS: measuring spoons, measuring cups, prep bowls, cutting board, serrated knife, small sharp knife, strainer, heavy-bottomed saucepan, mixing bowl, wooden spoon, whisk, can opener, grater, peeler, pot holders, timer

Put the onions and oil in a heavy-bottomed saucepan. Sauté for 5 minutes. Add the cayenne pepper, garlic, and ginger. Sauté for 2 minutes.

2 Add the vegetables and sauté for 2 more minutes.

3 Mix in the liquid and the tomatoes. Cover and **simmer** 10 minutes or until vegetables are tender. Add the okra and simmer 5 minutes.

4 In a mixing bowl, whisk ½ cup warm water and the peanut butter together until smooth. Add the peanut butter mixture to the pot and stir. Add the chickpeas and simmer for 10 minutes. Add salt and pepper to taste. Serve over rice.

Even Cooler!

For a more **authentic** meal, serve this stew with plantains. Use one plantain for each serving. Peel and cut each plantain into four pieces. Place them in a saucepan and cover them with cold water. Boil over medium-high heat until the plantains are tender. Drain them in a strainer. Put them in a bowl with 1 tablespoon of butter. Mash with a fork. Add salt and pepper to taste!

Tip

Peel the skins off the sweet potatoes before you cut them.

Juicy Jollof Rice

This excellent West African dish is a filling meal by itself!

MAKES 4 SERVINGS

TOOLS:

measuring spoons
measuring cups
prep bowls
mixing bowls

cutting board
serrated knife
small sharp knife
slotted spoon

heavy-bottomed saucepan
wooden spoon
can opener

strainer
pot holders
timer

1. Put the chicken and onion in a mixing bowl. Mix well using your clean hands.

2. Heat the canola oil in a heavy-bottomed saucepan over medium-high heat. Add the chicken mixture. Stir the chicken so it gets browned on all sides. When chicken is browned, remove it using a slotted spoon.
Put it in a bowl and set it aside.

3. Strain the juice from the can of tomatoes into a bowl. Chop the tomatoes into bite-size pieces.

4. Put the bell peppers and tomatoes in the saucepan. Sauté for 3 minutes. Add the tomato sauce, bay leaf, thyme, broth, rice, and chicken.

5. Cover the pan. **Simmer** over low heat for 45 to 60 minutes until the rice is done. Stir every 10 minutes to keep the rice from sticking to the pan. If all the liquid gets **absorbed**, add ¼ cup water. Add salt and pepper to taste and serve.

Even Cooler!

For a more **authentic** flavor, add ½ teaspoon cayenne pepper. Be careful! This pepper is very hot. Do not sniff the pepper. Be sure to wash your hands if you touch it.

Moroccan Carrot Salad

This simple and delicious salad is easy to make and great to eat!

MAKES 6 TO 8 SERVINGS

INGREDIENTS

- 1 pound carrots, peeled and cut into ½-inch slices
- 3 tablespoons lemon juice
- 3 tablespoons olive oil
- 1 teaspoon paprika
- 2 cloves garlic, minced
- 1 teaspoon ground cumin
- ½ cup cilantro, finely chopped
- salt
- ground pepper

TOOLS:
prep bowls
measuring spoons
measuring cups
cutting board
peeler
small sharp knife
4-quart saucepan
juicer
mixing bowls
whisk
wooden spoon
timer
strainer

1. Fill a 4-quart saucepan with water. Bring it to a boil. Add the carrots and cook for 5 minutes. Using the strainer, drain the carrots and let them cool. Put the carrots in a mixing bowl.

2. Put the remaining ingredients, except the cilantro, salt, and pepper in a small bowl. Whisk well. Pour the dressing over the carrots and mix.

3. Add the cilantro. Season with salt and pepper to taste. Mix well and chill.

Even Cooler!

For a spicier **version**, add ½ teaspoon hot pepper flakes or 1/8 teaspoon cayenne pepper.

Authentic Alecha

Make this Ethiopian veggie side dish spicy by adding hot peppers!

MAKES 6 SERVINGS

INGREDIENTS

6 small potatoes, peeled and thinly sliced

½ pound green beans, stems removed

4 carrots, peeled and thinly sliced

¼ cup canola oil

2 green or red bell peppers, thinly sliced

2 medium white onions, sliced into ½-inch crescents

1 tablespoon ginger root, grated

4 cloves garlic, minced

4 scallions, sliced

salt

ground pepper

TOOLS: prep bowls, measuring spoons, measuring cups, cutting board, small sharp knife, peeler, grater, strainer, 4-quart saucepan, heavy-bottomed saucepan, wooden spoon, pot holders, timer

1. Fill a 4-quart saucepan half full with water. Bring the water to a boil. Add the potatoes, beans, and carrots.

2. Cover and boil for 5 minutes. Drain the vegetables in a strainer and rinse with cold water. Set them aside.

3. Heat the canola oil in a heavy-bottomed saucepan. Add the peppers and onions. Sauté for 5 minutes. Add the ginger, garlic, scallions, and 1 teaspoon salt. Sauté for 5 minutes.

4. Add the drained vegetables and stir well. Cook over medium heat for 5 to 10 minutes. Stop when the vegetables are tender. Add salt and pepper to taste. Serve with rice or chapati.

Even Cooler!

For a spicier dish, add four Anaheim chili peppers. Prep these the same way you prep red or green peppers. Add them with the other peppers and onions. Like it even hotter? Add two sliced jalapeño peppers.

Tropical Fruit Salad

INGREDIENTS

3 bananas, peeled and cut into
½-inch slices

2 mangoes, peeled and cubed

2 cups pineapple, cubed

juice from 1 lime

½ cup shredded coconut

A delightful fresh fruit treat
that is great for a snack or dessert!

MAKES 8 SERVINGS

TOOLS: prep bowls   serrated knife   mixing bowl
cutting board   juicer   wooden spoon
small sharp knife   measuring cups   plastic wrap

1   Slice the bananas and cube the mangoes and pineapple.

2   Mix the bananas, mangoes, and pineapple together in a large bowl.
Add the lime juice and mix well.

3   Cover with plastic wrap and refrigerate for 1 hour. Sprinkle with coconut just before serving.

Even Cooler!

Try other tropical fruits such as guava, papaya, or avocado. You can also use pear, peach, melon, apple, grapefruit, orange or tangerine. Add 1 tablespoon of chopped fresh mint when you add the juice.

Explore the Foods of the Middle East

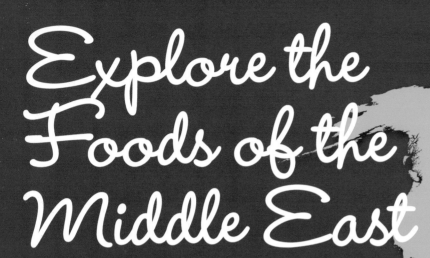

The Middle East is often called the cradle of civilization. People have lived there for more than 7,000 years! During this long history, recipes have been shared between many different people.

Today, many countries are informally a part of the Middle East. Most are in Asia near the Mediterranean Sea. This book includes recipes from Israel, Lebanon, Turkey, and Greece. Greece isn't always considered part of the Middle East. But Greek cooking includes many of the same ingredients and flavors!

Middle Eastern dishes often include nuts, olives, rice, and wheat. Chicken and lamb are the most popular meats. Yogurt and goat cheese are common too. Cinnamon, cumin, cayenne pepper, and paprika are popular spices. Are you ready for a tasty Middle Eastern adventure? Put on your apron, and off we go!

HOW DO YOU SAY THAT?

Bulgur (BUL-gur)

Hummus (HUHM-uhss)

Kofta (KOHF-tah)

Latke (LAHT-kuh)

Pilaf (PEE-lof)

Tabbouleh (tuh-BOO-luh)

Tahini (tuh-HEE-nee)

Tzatziki (tsah-TSEE-kee)

Ingredients

TOMATO

WHITE ONION

LEMONS

CARROTS

LEMONS

POTATOES

RADISHES

GARLIC

LETTUCE

GREEN PEPPER

FRESH PARSLEY

FRESH OREGANO

FRESH MINT

SCALLIONS

PITA BREAD

SALT

CUCUMBER

GROUND CINNAMON

GROUND CUMIN

WALNUTS

PAPRIKA

GROUND PEPPER

ALL-PURPOSE FLOUR

BULGUR WHEAT

CHICKEN BROTH

TAHINI

GROUND BEEF

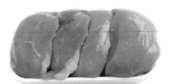

CHICKEN BREASTS

GREEK YOGURT

BUTTER

CHICKPEAS

LONG-GRAIN RICE

OLIVE OIL

PIE CRUST MIX

SUGAR

EGG

SEMISWEET CHOCOLATE CHIPS

HONEY

MILK

Middle Eastern Extras

Take your Middle Eastern cooking to the next level! The ideas on these pages will show you how.

TEMPTING TZATZIKI SAUCE

Makes 2 cups

INGREDIENTS

2 cucumbers, peeled, seeded, and diced
2 cups Greek yogurt
2 cloves garlic, minced
½ teaspoon salt
juice from 1 lemon
1 tablespoon dried or fresh mint
¼ cup olive oil (optional)

1 Mix all ingredients together.

2 Chill for at least 1 hour before serving.

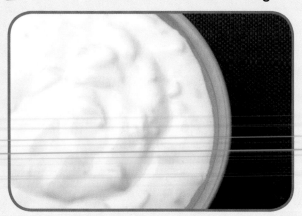

SIMPLE RICE PILAF

Makes 4 to 6 servings

INGREDIENTS

2 tablespoons butter
1 cup long-grain rice
1 teaspoon salt
2½ cups chicken broth

1 Melt the butter in a frying pan over medium-high heat. Add the rice and salt.

2 Stir constantly for about 2 minutes. The rice should start to turn golden and the butter should get foamy.

3 Slowly add the broth and stir. Bring to a boil over medium heat.

4 Cover the frying pan. Turn the heat to the lowest setting. Simmer for 25 to 30 minutes until the liquid is **absorbed**. Take the pan off the heat. Let it sit, covered, for 15 minutes. Stir the rice before serving.

CLASSIC HUMMUS DIP

Makes about 1½ cups

INGREDIENTS

1 15 oz can chickpeas, rinsed and drained
¼ cup tahini
2-3 cloves garlic, chopped (optional)
½ teaspoon salt
juice from 1 lemon
1/3 cup olive oil
1 tablespoon water
paprika

1 Put all the ingredients except the paprika in a blender. Blend until very smooth.

2 Put the hummus in a serving bowl. Sprinkle it with paprika. Serve with cut vegetables or pita bread.

LEBANESE TAHINA

Makes about 2 cups

INGREDIENTS

2 cloves garlic, minced
1 teaspoon salt
3/4 cup tahini
½ cup lemon juice
1 cup water
paprika
2 tablespoons chopped fresh parsley

1 Mix the garlic and salt together with a wooden spoon until it becomes a paste.

2 Mix in the tahini and the lemon juice.

3 Add the water slowly. Whisk until the mixture is smooth. If you like a thinner sauce, add more lemon juice and water.

4 Sprinkle the top with paprika and parsley before serving.

Harriet's Tasty Tabbouleh

This Lebanese salad is healthy and oh, so tasty!

MAKES 6 TO 8 SERVINGS

INGREDIENTS

- 2 cups water
- ¾ cup bulgur wheat
- 2 large bunches of parsley, finely chopped
- 1 cup finely chopped fresh mint
- ½ bunch scallions, finely chopped
- 2 large tomatoes, finely chopped
- 1 small dried onion, finely chopped
- ⅔ cup fresh lemon juice
- ½ cup olive oil
- salt and pepper to taste

TOOLS: prep bowls   serrated knife   saucepan   whisk
measuring cups   small sharp knife   strainer   wooden spoon
cutting board   juicer   mixing bowls

1. Boil the water in a saucepan. Turn off the heat and stir in the bulgur wheat. Let it stand for 30 minutes.

2. Rinse the bulgur wheat in strainer. Then drain and squeeze excess water out. Put it in a large mixing bowl. Add the parsley, mint, scallions, tomatoes, and dried onions. Mix well.

3. Whisk the olive oil and lemon juice together in a small bowl. Pour it over the bulgur wheat mixture.

4. Mix well. Add salt and pepper to taste.

Even Cooler!

For a more **authentic** tabbouleh, add ½ teaspoon ground cinnamon and increase parsley to 3 cups. Or spice it up and add ¼ teaspoon cayenne pepper.

Crispy Crunchy Veggie Salad

A delicious Israeli salad full of garden-fresh flavors!

MAKES 6 TO 8 SERVINGS

INGREDIENTS

- 2 large tomatoes, each sliced into 8 wedges
- 1 cucumber peeled, seeded, and cubed (½-inch pieces)
- 6 radishes, sliced thin
- 6 to 8 scallions, sliced thin
- 1 green pepper, cut into ¾-inch squares
- 2 carrots, sliced into ¼-inch slices
- ¼ cup olive oil
- 2 tablespoons lemon juice
- ¼ cup chopped fresh parsley
- ½ teaspoon salt
- ground pepper

TOOLS: prep bowls, cutting board, serrated knife, small sharp knife, measuring cups, measuring spoons, salad bowl, mixing bowl, whisk, spoon, two forks, peeler, pepper grinder, juicer

1 Put the tomatoes and all the vegetables in a **salad** bowl.

2 Whisk together the olive oil and lemon juice to make the dressing.

3 Pour the dressing over the vegetables. Use two forks to toss the salad. Add parsley and mix well.

4 Grind pepper over the top, then mix to blend. Add salt and pepper to taste. Chill for at least 1 hour before serving.

Even Cooler!

Make a Greek salad instead. **Omit** the radishes and carrots. Use 1 small red onion instead of the scallions. Slice the onion into thin wedges. Add ¼ cup pitted Kalamata olives. Crumble 2 ounces of feta cheese over the top before serving.

Tip

To peel and seed a cucumber, remove the peel with a vegetable peeler. Cut the cucumber in half the long way. Then use a spoon to scrape away the seeds.

Turkish Kofta Creations

This delightful Turkish favorite is just the thing for lunch or dinner!

MAKES 8 SERVINGS

INGREDIENTS

- 2 lb. ground beef
- ½ cup finely chopped fresh parsley
- ¼ cup finely chopped fresh mint
- 1 medium onion, grated
- 2 teaspoons ground cumin
- 1 teaspoon ground cinnamon
- 1 teaspoon salt
- ½ teaspoon ground pepper
- ¼ cup olive oil
- pita bread, cut in half
- onion, thinly sliced
- tomatoes, sliced
- lettuce
- tzatziki (see page 106)

TOOLS: prep bowls, measuring cups, measuring spoons, cutting board, small sharp knife, grater, mixing bowl, frying pan, spatula

1. Put the meat, parsley, mint, and grated onion in a mixing bowl. Mix with your hands. Make sure to wash them first! Add the cumin, cinnamon, salt, pepper, and olive oil. Mix well.

2. Divide the meat mixture into 16 equal portions. Roll each portion into a ball. Flatten each ball slightly to make a patty.

3. Put a little olive oil in a frying pan. Heat the oil over medium high heat. Add several patties. Fry them for 3 minutes on each side. Add more olive oil to the frying pan before cooking the remaining patties.

4. Serve the kofta patties on pita bread with sliced onion, tomatoes, lettuce, and tzatziki.

Even Cooler!

You can bake the kofta patties instead of frying them. Preheat the oven to 350 degrees. Put the kofta patties on a baking sheet. Bake for 12 to 15 minutes, until cooked all the way through.

Golden Potato Latkes

Make a great meal with this Israeli specialty and applesauce!

MAKES 8 CAKE

INGREDIENTS

4 medium potatoes, peeled

1 onion (about 2 inches across), grated

3 tablespoons all-purpose flour

½ teaspoon salt

1 egg, beaten

olive oil

TOOLS: prep bowls · peeler · grater · measuring spoons · measuring cups · fork · strainer · mixing bowl · frying pan · spatula · paper towels

1. Grate the potatoes using the largest holes on the grater. Put the potatoes in a strainer and press out the moisture. The potatoes hold a lot of moisture. Use your hands to squeeze out as much as you can.

2. Put the potatoes in a large bowl. Add the grated onion and mix with a fork. Add the flour, salt, and beaten egg. Mix well.

3. Heat ¼ inch of oil in a heavy frying pan over medium-high heat. After a few minutes, test the oil. Add a teaspoon of the potato mixture. If it starts to sizzle and brown right away, the oil is ready.

4. Put 1/3 cup of the potato mixture into the oil. Flatten it with a spatula to about ½ inch thick. Slip the spatula under the latke to keep it from sticking to the bottom of the frying pan. Fry 3 to 4 minutes until you see the edges turning golden brown.

5. Turn the latke over very carefully so the hot oil doesn't splash. Fry 3 to 4 minutes on the other side. Both sides should be golden brown. Put the latke on paper **towels** to drain.

6. Repeat Steps 4 and 5 to make more latkes. Serve them warm with applesauce or sour cream.

115

Greek Herbed Chicken

The simple Greek marinade makes the best-tasting chicken ever!

MAKES 4 TO 6 SERVINGS

INGREDIENTS

- ⅓ cup lemon juice
- ⅔ cup olive oil
- 4 cloves garlic, minced
- ¼ cup chopped fresh oregano
- 2 tablespoons chopped fresh parsley
- 1 teaspoon salt
- ½ teaspoon ground pepper
- 1 lb. chicken breasts, cut into serving pieces

TOOLS: whisk, prep bowls, juicer, measuring cups, measuring spoons, cutting board, small sharp knife, mixing bowls, wooden spoon, 9 x 9-inch baking dish, plastic wrap, pot holders, timer

1. Put the lemon juice, olive oil, and garlic in a small bowl. Whisk them together. Add the oregano, parsley, salt, and pepper and mix. This is the **marinade**.

2. Put the chicken pieces in a large bowl. Pour the marinade over chicken.

3. Mix to coat the chicken evenly with the marinade. Cover the bowl with plastic wrap. Refrigerate for at least two hours and up to 24 hours. Preheat the oven to 400 degrees.

4. Put the chicken and marinade into 9 x 9-inch baking dish. Bake for 30 minutes. Turn the oven down to 350 degrees. Bake for 30 to 45 minutes until chicken is cooked through. To check whether the chicken is done, cut into a thick piece. If it is not pink inside, the chicken is done.

Even Cooler!

Add other herbs to the marinade. Thyme and rosemary are good choices. Use 1 tablespoon of each. You can add up to 3 extra herbs.

Nummy Nut Wedges

A sweet and scrumptious Greek treat made with honey!

MAKES 8 TO 10 SERVINGS

INGREDIENTS

1 package pie crust mix
   (for 2 crusts)

½ cup sugar

3 to 4 tablespoons water

flour

1 cup walnuts, finely chopped

2 tablespoons honey

1 teaspoon ground cinnamon

1 teaspoon lemon juice

milk

½ cup semisweet chocolate
   pieces

1 teaspoon butter

TOOLS:

prep bowls	small sharp knife	rolling pin	wire rack
measuring cups	cutting board	glass pie dish	small saucepan
measuring spoons	mixing bowls	fork	
juicer	spoon	pastry brush	

1 Preheat the oven to 375 degrees.

2 In a medium bowl stir together pie crust mix and ¼ cup sugar. Add enough water to form a ball of dough. Divide the dough in half.

3 Sprinkle a little flour onto the counter. Using the rolling pin, roll each half of the dough into a 9-inch circle. Put one of the circles on an ungreased glass pie dish.

4 Combine the nuts, ¼ cup sugar, honey, cinnamon, and lemon juice in a bowl.

5 Spread the nut mixture over the dough on the glass pie dish. Put the other dough circle on top.

6 Use the tines of a fork to press around the edges of the dough.

7 Prick the top of the dough with a fork. Brush it with milk. Bake for 15 to 20 minutes or until **pastry** starts to brown. Put the pie on a wire rack.

8 Combine the chocolate pieces and butter in a small saucepan. Cook and stir over low heat just until melted. Drizzle the chocolate over the warm pie. Cut the pie into eight to ten wedges. Let them cool completely before serving.

Explore the Foods of China and Japan

Have you tried Chinese or Japanese food? These two countries are very different, but they have some things in common. For example, rice is the main food grown in each country. People there eat rice every day!

China is about the same size as the United States. But it has four times as many people! Almost half of Chinese workers are farmers. Japan is about the same size as California. It is made up of four main islands and many smaller ones. That's why the Japanese eat a lot of fish.

Chinese cooks often use a pan called a wok. Woks are used to cook food quickly over high heat, so vegetables stay brightly colored and crisp. Japanese cooks often use foods that are in season. That's when an ingredient is at its best! Are you ready for a tasty adventure? Put on your aprons and off we go!

120

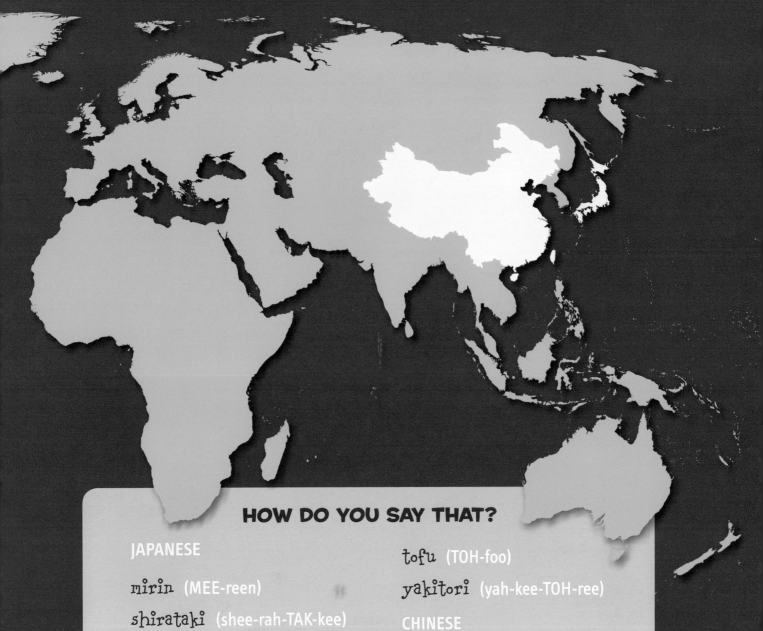

HOW DO YOU SAY THAT?

JAPANESE

mirin (MEE-reen)

shirataki (shee-rah-TAK-kee)

sunomono (soo-noh-MOH-noh)

sukiyaki (soo-kee-YAH-kee)

tofu (TOH-foo)

yakitori (yah-kee-TOH-ree)

CHINESE

bok choy (bok choi)

wok (wok)

Ingredients

BABY BOK CHOY

YELLOW ONION

SCALLIONS

CARROTS

MUNG BEAN SPROUTS

GINGER ROOT

GARLIC

FROZEN GREEN PEAS

GREEN PEPPER

RED PEPPER

CUCUMBER

BROWN SUGAR

FIRM TOFU

SHORT-GRAIN RICE

SUGAR

GROUND WHITE PEPPER

MUSHROOMS

**SESAME
SEEDS**

SALT

CASHEWS

PEANUTS

ALMONDS

ALL-PURPOSE FLOUR

GROUND CHICKEN

EGG

ANGEL HAIR PASTA

BONELESS, SKINLESS CHICKEN BREASTS

PEANUT BUTTER

LEAN BEEF STEAK

BREAD CRUMBS

SHIRATAKI NOODLES

BUTTER

SESAME OIL

OYSTER SAUCE

BAKING SODA

ALMOND EXTRACT

MIRIN

SOY SAUCE

CANOLA OIL

RICE VINEGAR

CORNSTARCH

Chinese and Japanese Extras

Take your Chinese and Japanese cooking to the next level! The ideas on these pages will show you how.

NO FUSS NOODLES!

Different kinds of pasta have different cook times. The suggested cooking time is always on the package.

1 Put 4 quarts of water in a heavy-bottomed saucepan. Add 1 tablespoon of salt and stir until it **dissolves**.

2 Bring the water to a boil over high heat. The entire surface of the water should be bubbling. Add the pasta and stir gently.

3 Wait for the water to begin boiling again. Then set the timer for the time shown on the package. Boil the pasta uncovered and stir it every few minutes. Make sure the pasta doesn't stick to the bottom of the pan.

4 Set a strainer in the sink. Pour the pasta into the strainer to drain. Serve immediately with sauce.

STUPENDOUS STEAMED RICE

Makes about 4 to 6 servings

INGREDIENTS
2½ cups short-grain white rice
3 cups cold water

1 Put the rice in a strainer and rinse.

2 Put the rinsed rice and water in a heavy, medium-size saucepan.

3 Bring to a boil over high heat. Cover the pan and turn the heat to medium. After 10 minutes, turn the heat to very low.

4 Cook for another 15 minutes. Do not peek! If you remove the cover the rice will not steam properly.

5 Turn off the heat and let the rice stand for 10 minutes. Before serving, fluff the rice with a fork or rubber spatula.

COOL CUCUMBER SUNOMONO

Makes about 4 to 6 servings

INGREDIENTS

2 tablespoons rice vinegar
2 teaspoons sugar
1 teaspoon water
1 tablespoon soy sauce
2 cucumbers, peeled, seeded and sliced thin
sesame seeds

1 Mix all the ingredients except the cucumbers in a small bowl. Stir until the sugar dissolves.

2 Put the cucumbers in a mixing bowl. Pour the sauce over the cucumbers. Stir to mix well.

3 Refrigerate for 1 hour before serving. Garnish with sesame seeds.

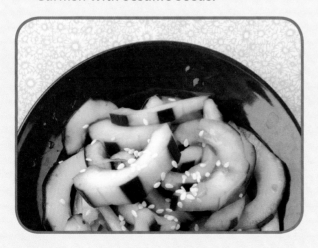

CHARMING CHINESE GREENS

Makes about 4 to 6 servings

INGREDIENTS

6 baby bok choy,
   stem end trimmed off
¼ cup oyster sauce
2 teaspoons water
1/8 teaspoon ground
   white pepper
1 tablespoon canola oil
2 cloves garlic, minced

1 Fill a heavy-bottomed saucepan half full with cold water. Bring the water to a boil over high heat. Carefully add the baby bok choy to the boiling water. After 30 seconds, remove the bok choy. Use a slotted spoon or a strainer with a long handle.

2 Drain the bok choy on paper **towels**. Mix the oyster sauce, water, and ground pepper together in a small bowl.

3 Heat the canola oil in a large frying pan. Add the minced garlic and sauté for 1 minute. Add the oyster sauce mixture. Stir and cook until the mixture is bubbly. Add the bok choy. Stir only until it is coated with the sauce. Serve on a large **platter**.

Sensational Sesame Noodles

These yummy noodles are easy to make and take!

MAKES 4 SERVINGS

INGREDIENTS

8 ounces angel hair pasta
3 tablespoons sesame seeds
¼ cup peanut butter
¼ cup water
3 tablespoons soy sauce
2 tablespoons sesame oil
1 tablespoon brown sugar
1 tablespoon rice vinegar
2 cloves garlic, minced
¼ teaspoon white pepper
2 scallions, chopped
½ red pepper, diced
1 cup fresh mung bean sprouts
¼ cup peanuts, chopped

TOOLS: prep bowls, measuring spoons, measuring cups, small sharp knife, cutting board, heavy-bottomed saucepan, strainer, baking sheet, blender, mixing bowl, wooden spoon, timer, pot holders, 4 dinner bowls

1. Preheat the oven to 275 degrees. Follow the instructions on page 126 to cook the angel hair pasta.

2. Rinse the cooked pasta with cold water. Stir to separate the strands. Leave it in the strainer to drain.

3. Spread the sesame seeds on a baking sheet. Put them in the oven for 5 minutes. The seeds will turn a light golden brown.

4. Put the peanut butter, water, soy sauce, sesame oil, brown sugar, rice vinegar, garlic, white pepper, and sesame seeds in a blender. Blend until smooth.

5. Put the drained pasta in a large bowl. Pour the blended ingredients over it.

6. Stir gently with a large spoon until the pasta is evenly coated with the dressing. Divide the pasta into four bowls.

7. **Garnish** each bowl with scallions, red pepper, bean sprouts, and peanuts.

Chicken Meatball Yakitori

See why snacks on skewers are so popular in Japan!

MAKES 6 TO 8 SERVINGS

INGREDIENTS

¼ cup mirin

1 tablespoon sugar

½ cup soy sauce

1 pound ground chicken

1 egg yolk

2 teaspoons ginger root, peeled and minced

1 tablespoon soy sauce

½ cup bread crumbs

6 scallions, finely chopped

canola oil

TOOLS:

prep bowls	cutting board	baking sheet	wooden skewers
measuring spoons	small saucepan	pastry brush	
measuring cups	wooden spoon	timer	
small sharp knife	mixing bowls	pot holders	

1 Preheat the oven to 400 degrees.

2 Put the mirin, sugar, and ½ cup soy sauce in a small saucepan. Heat over medium heat, stirring until the sugar **dissolves**. Let the mixture **simmer** for 10 minutes, stirring occasionally. The mixture thickens to syrup as it cooks.

3 Remove the pan from the heat. Pour the mixture into a small bowl. Set it aside. Put all the remaining ingredients except canola oil in a mixing bowl. Mix the ingredients with your hands. Make sure you wash them first!

4 Get your hands wet. Roll small pieces of the meat mixture between your hands to make meatballs. They should be about 1 inch across.

5 Grease a baking sheet with a small amount of canola oil. Put three meatballs on each wooden skewer. Set the skewers on the baking sheet.

6 Bake for 5 minutes. Remove the baking sheet from the oven and turn the skewers over. Make sure you use a pot holder! Bake for 5 more minutes. Take the meatballs out of the oven.

7 Turn oven temperature down to 325 degrees. Brush the meatballs with the sauce. Bake for 3 more minutes to heat the sauce.

Tip

To get just the egg yolk, crack the egg into a small bowl. Use a slotted spoon to gently lift the yolk from the white.

Spectacular Sukiyaki

This fast-cooking Japanese dish is too good to miss!

MAKES 4 TO 6 SERVINGS

INGREDIENTS

1 cup water

½ cup soy sauce

½ cup mirin

2 tablespoons sugar

3 tablespoons canola oil

1 pound lean beef steak, cut into thin strips

1 large yellow onion sliced into moon shapes

3 carrots, peeled and sliced into thin slices on the diagonal

8 mushrooms, cut in half

1 package of shirataki noodles

1 14-ounce package firm tofu, cut into 1-inch cubes

6 scallions, sliced into 1-inch pieces

TOOLS: prep bowls
measuring spoons
measuring cups
small sharp knife

cutting board
small saucepan
mixing bowls
wooden spoon

large, heavy-bottomed pot
tongs
kitchen scissors

peeler
strainer
timer
pot holders

1. Put the water, soy sauce, mirin, and sugar in a small saucepan. Cook over high heat. Stir with a wooden spoon until the sugar **dissolves**. When the mixture boils, remove it from the heat and let it cool. This is the sauce.

2. Make sure the prepared vegetables are handy. You will need to add them to the pot quickly.

3. Put the canola oil in a large, heavy-bottomed pot. Heat over medium-high heat. Add the beef. Sauté for 2 minutes. Use tongs to turn the meat. Move the meat to one side of the pan.

4. Add the onions and carrots. Keep each ingredient in its own part of the pot. Sauté for 3 minutes. Add the mushrooms.

5. Stir the vegetables to keep them from sticking to the bottom of the pot. Add the sauce and bring to a boil.

6. Drain the shirataki noodles. Put the noodles in a bowl. Cut them into several pieces with clean kitchen scissors. Add the shirataki noodles, tofu, and scallions to the pot.

7. Cook until the meat is no longer pink and the vegetables are hot. The total cooking time should be about 10 minutes.

8. Serve in large bowls with steamed rice on the side.

Even Cooler!

Try using other vegetables such as thinly sliced potatoes, spinach, shitake mushrooms, enoki mushrooms, leeks, or Napa cabbage.

Cashew Chicken Stir Fry

This popular Chinese restaurant dish is even better when you make it at home!

MAKES 4 SERVINGS

INGREDIENTS

- 2 tablespoons oyster sauce
- 1 tablespoon soy sauce
- 1/8 teaspoon ground white pepper
- 2 teaspoons sesame oil
- water
- 1 boneless skinless chicken breast.
- 2 tablespoons cornstarch
- 2 tablespoons canola oil
- 1 bunch scallions, cut into 1-inch slices
- 1 green pepper, cleaned and cut into thin strips
- 6 thin slices peeled ginger root
- ½ cup cashews

TOOLS:
prep bowls
measuring spoons
measuring cups
small sharp knife

cutting board
whisk
paper towels
mixing bowl

wooden spoon
wok or large frying pan
timer

pot holders

1. Put the oyster sauce, soy sauce, white pepper, 1 teaspoon sesame oil, and ¼ cup water in a mixing bowl. Whisk well.

2. Rinse the chicken and pat it dry using paper **towels**. Cut the chicken into cubes.

3. Put the cornstarch, 2 teaspoons water, and 1 teaspoon sesame oil in a large bowl. Whisk until smooth. Add the chicken pieces. Mix well to coat the chicken. **Marinate** the chicken for 15 minutes.

4. Heat the canola oil in a large frying pan or wok over medium high heat. Use a wooden spoon to remove the chicken from the marinade. Put the chicken in the pan. Sauté for 10 minutes.

5. Add the scallions, green pepper, and ginger. Sauté for 5 minutes.

6. Add the cashews and oyster sauce mixture. Stir to coat all the ingredients with the sauce. Cook for 5 minutes, stirring often. The sauce will thicken a little bit as it cooks. Test one piece of chicken to be sure it is cooked in the middle. If there is no pink color, the chicken is done.

7. Serve over steamed white rice.

Chinese Fried Rice

Leftover rice becomes a delicious meal!

MAKES 6-8 SERVINGS

INGREDIENTS

- 2 tablespoons canola oil
- 3 cloves garlic, minced
- 1 cup frozen green peas
- 8 mushrooms, sliced
- 6 cups rice, cooked and cooled
- 3 tablespoons soy sauce
- 1/8 teaspoon ground white pepper
- 5 scallions, chopped
- 2 eggs, lightly beaten
- 1 cup mung bean sprouts

TOOLS: prep bowls · measuring spoons · measuring cups · small sharp knife · cutting board · mixing bowl · wooden spoon · wok or large frying pan · timer · pot holders · whisk

1. Heat the canola oil in a wok or a large frying pan. When the oil is hot, add the garlic. Sauté over medium-high heat for 2 minutes.

2. Add the peas and mushrooms. Sauté for 2 minutes. Add the rice and stir well using a wooden spoon.

3. Add in the soy sauce, white pepper, and scallions. Continue to cook and stir for 5 minutes.

4. Make a well in the middle of the rice. Pour the eggs into the well. After about 30 seconds, cover the eggs with the rice. After 1 minute, stir to blend in the eggs.

5. Continue stirring until the eggs are cooked. Add the bean sprouts and stir to mix before serving.

Even Cooler!

Make chicken fried rice! Cut a boneless skinless chicken breast into small cubes. Add the chicken after Step 1. Sauté for 5 minutes before doing Step 2.
Or make **shrimp** fried rice! Use eight cooked, medium shrimp. Remove the shells and tails. Cut the shrimp into small chunks. Add it to the fried rice in Step 2.

Crunchy Almond Cookies

Enjoy these sweet treats after a nutritious dinner!

INGREDIENTS

- 2 cups all-purpose flour
- ½ teaspoon salt
- 1 cup sugar
- ½ teaspoon baking soda
- 12 tablespoons butter, softened at room temperature
- 1 egg, slightly beaten
- 1½ teaspoons almond extract
- 36 whole almonds
- 1 egg yolk
- 2 teaspoons water

MAKES 3 DOZEN COOKIES

TOOLS: prep bowls, measuring spoons, measuring cups, mixing bowl, whisk, slotted spoon, pastry brush, baking sheet, wire baking rack, timer, pot holders, hand mixer, airtight container

1. Preheat the oven to 325 degrees. Lightly grease the baking sheet.

2. Stir flour, salt, sugar, and baking soda together in a large bowl. Add softened butter. Mix with a hand mixer until the mixture looks like crumbs. Blend in the beaten egg and almond extract.

3. Wash your hands. Then squish the mixture together until it forms a smooth dough.

4. Roll a small piece of the dough into a 1-inch ball. Put it on the baking sheet. Gently press down with your fingers to flatten it just a little. Repeat this with the rest of the dough. Place the cookies 2 inches apart on the baking sheet.

5. In a small bowl, whisk together the egg yolk and 2 teaspoons water. Use a pastry brush to lightly brush each cookie with the egg mixture. Press an almond in the center of each cookie.

6. Bake for 20 to 24 minutes. The cookies are done when they are lightly golden on top.

7. Remove the cookies from the baking sheet. Set them on a wire baking rack to cool. Store them in an airtight container.

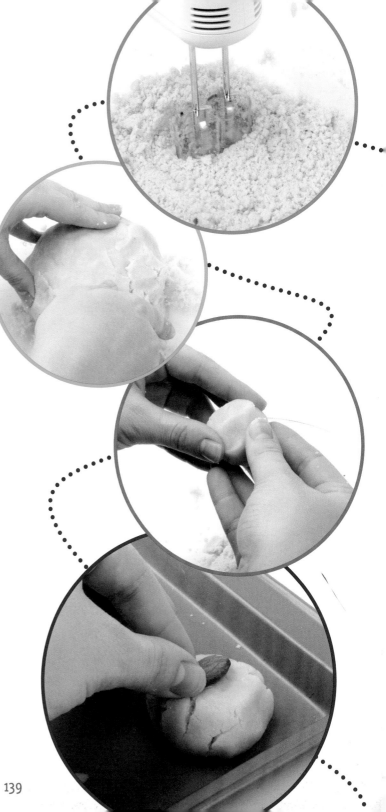

Glossary

absorb – to soak up or take in.

authentic – real or true.

available – able to be had or used.

conventionally – in the usual way.

cousin – the child of your aunt or uncle.

crispy – hard, thin, and easy to break.

culture – the behavior, beliefs, art, and other products of a particular group of people.

dangerous – able or likely to cause harm or injury.

delicious – very pleasing to taste or smell.

dice – cut into small cubes.

discard – to throw away.

dissolve – to become part of a liquid.

garnish – to add small amounts of food to finish a dish.

grocery store – a place where you buy food items.

improvise – to use what you have on hand to make something.

insert – to stick something into something else.

kosher – prepared according to Jewish law.

marinade – a sauce that food is soaked in before cooking. To marinate something means to soak it in a marinade.

medical – having to do with doctors or the science of medicine.

nutritious – good for people to eat.

omit – to leave out.

optional – something you can choose, but is not required.

pastry – dough used to make pies and other baked goods.

pesticide – a chemical used to kills bugs and other pests.

platter – a large plate.

pork – meat that comes from a pig.

poultry – birds, such as chickens or turkeys, raised for eggs or meat.

salad – a mixture of raw vegetables usually served with a dressing.

shrimp – a small shellfish often caught for food.

simmer – to stew gently at a soft boil.

substitution – the act of replacing one thing with another.

synthetic – man-made rather than found in nature.

thermometer – a tool used to measure temperature.

towel – a cloth or paper used for cleaning or drying.

version – a different form or type from the original.

Index